ON THE BORDER

Living with Borderline Personality Disorder

AMANDA READ

On the Border: Living with Borderline Personality Disorder © Amanda Read 2020

First published with permission in 2020 by Disruptive Publishing

>17 Spencer Avenue
>Deception Bay, QLD 4508
>Australia
>www.disruptivepublishing.com.au

Edited by Jacki Ferro at www.rawmemoirs.com

All rights reserved. No part of this book may be reproduced or transmitted in any form or by any means, electronic or mechanical, including photocopying, recording or by any information storage and retrieval system, without prior written permission from the author.

The information in this book is not intended as a substitute for professional or medical advice. Neither the author nor publisher can accept any responsibility for any illness, injuries, damages or losses suffered as a result of following any information herein.

Content warning: readers should be advised that some of the material within this book could cause distress. The contents of this book describe real events that include themes of death, self-harm, suicide, mental health and disorders, abuse (including sexual), violent encounters with police, and more. If whilst reading you find yourself feeling distressed, you can find links to health resources and helplines at youth and adult mental health services in each state, such as Headspace, as well as by searching for services online.

Some names have been changed to protect the personal privacy of the people mentioned in this book.

National Library of Australia Cataloguing-In-Publication data is available at www.trove.nla.gov.au

ISBN#: 978-0-6489671-6-3

To my son, Jamie

Acknowledgments

Thanks to all of those who've encouraged me to find my voice as a consumer representative of mental health services.

I would especially like to acknowledge those who saw the real Jamie. They saw what other people didn't get to see. Particular mention to a psychologist of many years who once said, "I've worked with hundreds of kids and some are in your heart and you never forget them. Your son Jamie will live on in my heart." One worker in youth detention once told me that Jamie was not like the other kids there. "He has a heart of gold."

I treasure and take comfort from these kind words.

My greatest thanks to my children, from whom I have learned so much.

Thank you for allowing me to share some of your most intimate stories here.

I acknowledge the Australian Aboriginal and Torres Strait Islander peoples of this nation.

I acknowledge the traditional custodians of the lands on which I have lived and conducted my business. I pay my respects to ancestors and Elders, past and present. I am committed to honouring Australian Aboriginal and Torres Strait Islander peoples' unique cultural and spiritual relationships with the land, waters and seas, and their rich contribution to society.

Contents

Acknowledgments — 5
Author's Note — 9
Contact the Author — 13
Don't Cry for Me, Argentina — 15

Part One: The Silent Generation

Good Girls Don't Talk — 23
On the Outside Looking In — 31
Crash — 37
I Want to Learn a Love Song Full of Happy Things — 47
Loving in the Shadows — 59
Shifting Sands — 69

Part Two: The Flower, the Lion, the Monkey, and the Gift

Parenting Prophesy — 77
The Flower — 79
The Lion — 83
The Monkey — 89
The Gift — 93
Extreme Parenting and Stolen Joys — 101

Part Three: For the Love of Jamie

Something's Happened to the Boy — 109
Kids that Age Don't try to Kill Themselves — 117
Brother — 125
… Just Another Junkie — 135
Final Days — 145
Sharing My Lessons — 153

Author's Note

I am Amanda Read – mother to four children, grandmother to nine, and great grandmother to two great grandchildren. I work with families as this is my passion. It means so much to me that every family should have the compassion, understanding, support and strength to survive what is thrown at them. We live in a changing world and we often parent with guilt, struggling to meet the needs of our kids and to prepare them for a world that we are not sure we understand ourselves.

I achieved my Bachelor of Social Science in 2006 after twelve long years of study, during which, as for many contemporary mums, competing priorities meant that I constantly juggled my life, family, work and study. Achieving my goals was made all the more difficult by the effects on my family of Borderline Personality Disorder (BPD).

The other big challenge for me was to resist succumbing to mental illness myself. I exhibit traits of emotional instability – a common experience for young people who grow up with a parent who has a mental illness. I became a parent very young. I had nurtured my sisters and so fell into what I knew best, and had a child at sixteen. This is my story about the challenges I have faced.

My family's story is one of resilience, impacted by inter-generational trauma and mental illness. This trauma affects our everyday lives, our loves, and our ability to maintain a sense of security, safety, and good mental health. There are times when we have failed to cope, and times of absolute triumph.

With little community awareness and support in Australia in the 1960s and 70s, combined with shame, a lack of medical knowledge around mental illness, and living with a mother who struggled to survive, such was the context of my childhood. Add to this a father who held rigid, traditional beliefs about marriage and gender roles, and who was raising three daughters. Our father also lacked any understanding of differences in culture, and he found it difficult to express or witness strong displays of emotion. Our family life was a true recipe for disaster.

My story describes how pervasive mental illness can be in its ability to wreck relationships. Conversely, this is also the story of how we all have somehow maintained our connections and love for one another. Despite the effects of this illness, I hope that those who know us have been touched by the wonderful richness of our personalities. Some may have even found us a tiny bit charming or delightful, and may value and admire the way our lives have entwined.

Borderline Personality Disorder is defined in the *Diagnostic and Statistical Manual of Mental Disorders (DSM–IV)* by the American Psychiatric Association (2000):

> *The defining criteria of Borderline Personality Disorder (BPD) is a pervasive pattern of instability of interpersonal relationships, self-image, and affects, and marked impulsivity that begins by early adulthood and is present in a variety of contexts, as indicated by five (or more) of the following:*
>
> - *Frantic efforts to avoid real or imagined abandonment.*
> - *A pattern of unstable and intense interpersonal relationships characterized by alternating between extremes of idealization and devaluation.*
> - *Identity disturbance: markedly and persistently unstable self-image or sense of self; or sense of long-term goals; or career choices, types of friends desired, or values preferred.*

- *Impulsivity in at least two areas that are potentially self-damaging: for example, spending, sex, substance abuse, and binge eating.*
- *Recurrent suicidal behavior, gestures, or threats, or self-mutilating behavior.*
- *Affective instability: marked shifts from baseline mood to depression, irritability, or anxiety, usually lasting a few hours and only rarely more than a few days.*
- *Chronic feelings of emptiness.*
- *Inappropriate, intense anger or difficulty controlling anger; frequent displays of temper.*
- *Transient, stress-related paranoid ideation or severe dissociative symptoms.*

In 2013, the APA released the DSM-V, which, I understand, included big changes to the way personality disorders are diagnosed. Personality disorders are now seen as "adaptive failures", rather than pervasive patterns. I prefer this view, as I see my life and the lives of those around me as a struggle. We cope with things in the best way we can, and we survive in spite of these things that appear "odd" to others.

Childhood memories are strange, and I am sure that my family may challenge my recollections. All I can say is that they are mine – my perceptions and how I have made sense of the world. If any of my memories are painful or cause distress, for that I am sorry – that is not my intention. I wanted to share my personal struggle to maintain balance in my life in the shadow of Borderline Personality Disorder.

Contact the Author

Although Bali is her spiritual home and the place she goes to for replenishment, Amanda lives north of Brisbane with her husband. Her children and grandchildren live across Australia and, like other close family, come and go intermittently, as her home is the family's safe place to fall.

Reach out to Amanda at mandir02@yahoo.com.au and follow her events and journey on her Facebook page On the Border – For the Love of James.

Don't Cry for Me, Argentina

I was born in the small country town of Manjimup, Western Australia – Karri Country to Aboriginal people – to parents who were still settling into a country that was not their birthplace. Both had brought with them extremely different histories and experiences, and some would say that they were obviously mismatched. As children, both migrated to Australia with their families, seeking new lives. As with all families, my story is only part of a much bigger, rich tapestry of triumph and tragedy.

My mother and grandmother came from a Latin American culture steeped in emotion, passion, and rebelliousness. They left their homeland to live in refugee camps, before arriving at their final destination of Fremantle, WA. My Nonna Lidia was a very young wife and mother of four children. She had followed her husband from her home in Argentina to his conflict-torn country of Yugoslavia. Their final contact with her family resulted in the physical assault of Lidia's father, my great grandfather, as he pleaded with his son-in-law (my grandfather) not to take his daughter to another country.

As I understand it, caught up in his Eastern European country's attempt to repatriate their countrymen with promises of a bright new future, my grandfather Marco took his young family and returned them to his home where he was in the merchant navy. Marco had earlier left the country illegally, due to his political beliefs. In the late 1940s, the Yugoslav government was encouraging all expats to come home because WWII was over, and life was improving. After being there a short time, however, grandfather felt that nothing had changed politically. He learned that what the government was saying wasn't true. After a few weeks, his disenchantment and passionate political views saw him take the dramatic step of jumping on a ship and leaving everything, including his young family, behind. To put this into context, my grandfather was always a paranoid man. To this day, our family does not know where he went, but his personality was one of suspicion and distrust of authorities.

Shortly after grandfather left, Lidia was arrested and interrogated by the Yugoslav authorities. She was left in a strange country, not knowing the language nor understanding the money, and having to bear the wrath of authorities who could not believe that she did not know where her husband was. Lidia and her children were left at the whim of people who did not always have their best interests at heart. My mother and her siblings suffered greatly during this time, enduring extreme poverty, hunger and deprivation. They lived in refugee camps in Yugoslavia, then moved to Italy and lived in refugee camps there. Nonna waited till I was eighteen to tell me this story, as she didn't wish for me to hate my grandfather. Nonna said that all of her children had desperately wanted to return to Argentina and that, although they were called refugee camps, in Yugoslavia they effectively lived in prisoner-of-war camps.

A legendary story in our home was how, in the late 1940s to early 1950s, Eva Peron and her foundation had worked tirelessly to repatriate their fellow countrymen and women. I was eighteen before Nonna finally felt she could tell me her story, and how she had survived this time in her life. Perhaps the release of Evita triggered Nonna to share stories of her earlier life with me. Prior to then, she would only say, as many migrants do, "We are so lucky to live here in Australia."

Stuck in the refugee camps in Italy, all of Lidia's children had desperately wanted to return to Argentina. They missed the family they remembered. Nonna reached out and organised to have herself and her children repatriated. As suddenly as he had disappeared, my grandfather then reappeared. Reunited with my grandfather and, despite pleas from the children to continue with plans to return to Argentina and the family they remembered, Lidia decided that her place was beside her husband, so they made their way to Australia.

Sponsored by my grandad Marco's relations, my mother's childhood family began their new life in the market gardens of Spearwood, a southern suburb of Perth. As a beautiful sixteen-year-old, my mum featured in the local newspaper, about three months after they arrived. Making note of her ability to speak four languages fluently, including English, at such a young age, the media article seemed to indicate that she had settled comfortably into Australian life.

Unfortunately, such was not the case for her mother, Nonna Lidia. Nonna's life was made difficult due to both her gender and long-held cultural norms around women's roles, and discrimination from "dinky-di" Australians. My grandfather's brother owned market gardens in Spearwood, and Lidia became the breadwinner, working long hours, growing all sorts of vegetables, like tomatoes, onions, lettuce and potatoes. Nonna often shared with me stories of the cultural roles of women in Yugoslavia. The women worked hard, often doing many tasks, like working in the fields all day with babies strapped to their backs, then led the mule loaded up with the harvest they had gathered, and knitting socks as they walked along. Meanwhile, the men could often be found playing cards and drinking vino in the shade.

Nonna often expressed to me her guilt about her young, Aussie born daughter having to live in a shed at the back of the market garden. Their "home" had dirt floors, and the children were left in the care of my grandad who had no qualms about children becoming dirty. It broke Nonna's heart to live in such conditions, and she once told me that, even in the camps where they had nothing, she had her pride and kept an immaculate home. She described how she had made doilies for the shelves out of old newspapers, by folding and decorating them with patterns that she cut out, and how each scrap of clothing was cut down and re-fashioned for whatever useful items the home needed. And all this without the use of a sewing machine. This control over Nonna's environment lived on. Right up until she was in her nineties, Nonna Lidia kept a pristine home.

Eventually, the family moved to the south-western mill town of Quinninup where my grandfather Marco was able to gain work in the timber industry that flourished there in the late 1950s. This small town was where my mother and father met.

My father's mother, Evelyn (known as Evie), has told me that, prior to the war and before they had children, her husband, my British grandfather, was the an active member of the Communist party both in England and in Australia. He was well educated and, as the war approached, he apparently gave speeches in London's Hyde Park. After becoming a father, however, he decided to give this all away because he did not want to risk his children's lives. So, my father's family migrated to Australia paying their own fares. My dad had his 9th birthday on the boat bound for Australia and recalls the racism directed at him on his arrival in Austraila.

It seems, as I ponder the decisions made, and with grandparents deceased, that I can only make sense of this by imagining my English grandfather as a passionate and political man who, having denied his beliefs and values, was left with a void in his life. This void caused him to seek a life in farming, something he knew nothing about. Perhaps, the attraction for him was the seeming lack of class-consciousness in Australian society at the time. Then again, perhaps this is fanciful thinking on my behalf.

My paternal grandmother, Nana Evie, spoke of receiving a decent education and working as a secretary before marriage. They then lived in a modern housing estate in England while my grandfather ran his own successful house building and painter-decorating business. Nana has told me that she made many friends in the estate, and that she had everything she wanted.

One day, my grandfather arrived home to tell Evelyn that he had sold the business and that they were moving to Australia, a place he had visited previously and where his brother lived, in Melbourne. Nana told me of her shock and dismay at arriving to confront the isolation and lack of basic amenities of Diamond Tree in south-western WA. As Nana said, "I'd never even washed a hanky myself!" I believe that this move signalled the death knell of my grandparents' marriage.

My birth was an exciting event in our family, as I was the first grandchild on my mother's side. My mum, who had been cherished and doted on by her Argentinian mother in an attempt to protect her from the harsh life that she herself had encountered as a mother, told stories of me as this amazing, cherub-like girl-child who loved her food and was so good that she would always wash her hands on the cloth hanging by the sink. This would, in later years, be qualified by her, "I don't know what happened to you!" Well, some things never change, and I still love my food.

Moving from the idolised princess who would have her hair and feet washed by her mother even late into her teens, Mum found that married life was not the ideal that she'd expected, and she did not find it easy. With each consecutive birth, my mother's mental health deteriorated, along with her marriage, and her ability to manage the demands of three young children.

Mum seemed obsessed with providing our father a son, and we grew up feeling that we were second-best to males. This fact is denied by my father, but it was later reconfirmed when, years later, he had another child – finally, a male.

One thing that my Mum really enjoyed was working outside of the home, and Dad always said that she was at her best when working. In the 1960s, however, it was difficult to find employers willing to take on married women, let alone mothers, and gender roles in the home were more fixed than they are today.

Part One

The Silent Generation

Chapter One

Good Girls Don't Talk

Although we had moved around often, Silas Street in East Fremantle was home. Years later, it would be resumed for a new highway, and so, my childhood home is long gone, along with the other character homes of that area. Luckily, the wonderful George Street terrace houses remain, preserved as a historical precinct. As I walk down there today, I recall the fish and chip shop, a regular haunt on Friday nights, and the delightful corner store that sold the most amazing range of lollies, when 1c bought you four sweets.

Our home backed onto the Old Royal George Hotel and, in those days, they still had working stables. We often heard the horses, which I have feared to this day. The large block was our playground, but we were also free to walk and explore our suburb, visiting shops and our friends' houses. Those were times of not too many worries.

I do recall, however, one time when I had been fighting with my parents. I decided to run away, so I packed my little school case and stomped off up the hill. As I approached the hotel, I suddenly grew fearful. It was early evening, and a few of the locals stumbled out of the pub, no doubt having enjoyed a few ales after work. I have always felt scared around people who are drinking or those affected by alcohol. On this day, my heart was beating really fast and I started to shake. I turned and ran straight back home. That incident threatened my sense of security. Although alcohol was not regularly used in our home, I can remember friends who would visit and drink, and who often ended up arguing.

Growing up was painful for me and, looking back, I think that I might have been a child who would be classed as "having a difficult temperament". Some might argue that I've carried that trait through to the present. On many occasions in my life, I have made moral judgments, and I have this permanent focus on social justice, the origin of which remains unclear. This trait was a constant source of much consternation for the adults around me. I have always empathised when I've sensed that women's rights are not being upheld, I dislike alcohol or being in the company of drinkers, and, by the time I was twelve, I was engaging in arguments around politics, with a markedly left-wing slant, much to my family's horror.

My earliest, surely selected as the happiest, memory from my childhood was when I started school. Grade One at East Fremantle State Primary School began in a beautiful limestone building, characteristic of many of the historic buildings in Fremantle. Set high on the hill, with views to the wonderful coastline and harbour, I loved this school and I loved learning – it awakened something in me. I loved my teacher, too. Surely, she was the kindest person in the whole world, and I learned to gain attention by being compliant. As a good student, I was rewarded beyond my dreams with a final report that featured the comment, "Amanda came top of the class". *Wow!* This was so great, and it made me get noticed. Even at home, I became visible for my achievements, which were proudly shared among the extended family.

I recall the old school bell that only the most trusted students got to ring to signal the end of classes and breaks, and the milk in little bottles that I refused to drink as it tasted yucky. I also fondly remember the parades around the playground, marching "1, 2, 3", round and round. These memories bring me comfort, as their rhythm was consistent and timeless, and they made me feel a part of something bigger than me. Even when the hot sun beat down on us, nothing marred my first, triumphant year of school.

I had a good number of school friends, and I certainly would not say that I was unpopular, yet, at times, I felt alone and isolated, as if in a bubble. It is like my emotions that were big, bright and bold had become whitewashed, or perhaps that was the earliest signs of me wanting to block many things out.

During school holidays, we travelled south-west, through Manjimup and along the Cheannybearup Road, just a gravel track, lined with tall trees that cast speckled shadows, to my uncle's (my father's brother) West Pemberton farm where they grew many potatoes, but also cauliflower, peas and other vegetables. My Uncle Stan was a tall and hardworking but playful man who would often sit with me in the kitchen and debate my passionate political statements. Uncle Stan was tolerant of my "strike" when I refused to go out on the potato harvester until I was promised a financial reward. I owe a great thanks to my wonderful uncle and to my dad who both indulged such a naive and idealistic young girl. These experiences helped me to formulate my arguments, and to see myself as a person whose opinions mattered. As a girl, I felt extremely privileged to have this gift given to me.

Uncle Stan died in early 2014. I wrote and read the eulogy at his funeral. I based it on a letter I had written him before he passed away. As a young child, my son Jamie who was mischievous and game would challenge this brawny, over six-foot-something farmer. Uncle Stan responded, "I will knock your block off!" Thus, started a game in which Jamie did this every time he saw his great uncle, and they always laughed together. Visits to "Diamond Tree" farm where my Nana Evelyn lived invoke images of rolling green paddocks, dairy cows loping along tracks, mushrooms growing out of cow pats, and that house with the wonderful hay shed where we built cubbies, and played hide and seek. This small settlement also featured a sawmill, and the smell of freshly sawn timber permeated the air – Ah, wonderful memories. Cooking with "Evie", as Nana was known, among the mainly Italian residents of Diamond Tree, was a treat for me. I loved Nana for her serenity and compassion, and for the way she made me feel special. She taught me so much.

I remember family gatherings when we made Italian sausages. Oh, they were such prized possessions – boiled up while they were fresh, or hung up to dry for eating later. The slaughter of a large pig with sharp knives was followed by stretching sausage skins and scrunching them over the mincer pipe. We watched as the mince was fed into the long skins, growing quickly. The smells and sounds, a mixture of fresh meat, spices, and lots of laughter and fun, made it a fabulous community event.

Earliest memories with mother's mother, Nonna Lidia, include time spent with my aunty, only five years older than me, and the relative freedom that such a small and safe community offered in those days. Other times, Nonna Lidia and I baked cakes together. I was always fascinated with how she could cream the butter and sugar by hand, furiously beating them with her wooden spoon. How I loved to stick my finger in the bowl and taste the smooth, sweet delight before the flour was added. I remember Nonna's home as basic, yet immaculately clean, with a beautiful vegie garden and chickens out the back.

During my early years, both sides of my family engaged in social and recreational activities, and there was a sense of one big family, all drawn together by similar circumstances, without division about who belonged where. Nana Evie's new partner, Emilio, had a lease on a property, now in the D'entrecasteaux National Park. Broke Inlet, with its windswept shoreline, was an amazing and Idyllic natural adventure playground for us children. Set on the riverbank, a short crossing from the inlet led to days of boating, fishing, swimming, and water-skiing. When we tired of that, there was bush walking, playing games with the cousins or just relaxing. I remember times when our small shack housed up to twenty-two people. While we set up several tents, we shared meals together. We had to light the kerosene fridges, gather firewood, light fires, and de-cobweb and sweep out the cabin when we arrived. All of these perfect memories are only marred by the need to slap your legs and arms to avoid the bites of March flies.

What changed from that time, and when exactly it changed, I am not sure. But I remember my first experience of abuse, aimed directly at me. Mum had bouts of being unwell – periods of hospitalisation in psychiatric care – and other times being present in our lives and trying to parent. Family members came and went to care for us while she was ill. We moved house often and for short periods, too, as Dad chased employment.

Within my mind, I hold the distinct memory of a visit from an uncle in whose presence I never felt comfortable. On the outside, he seemed attentive and kind to us, but I felt tense around him. I don't remember the night well, or where my parents were, or why my uncle was there, but I remember lying in the front bedroom, in my parents' bed, in our old house in Silas Street. My uncle entered the room. He sat on the bed, talking and stroking my hair. After a while, he stood up and unzipped his pants, showing me his hard penis. He asked me to put it in my mouth. I complied, as I was a good girl, and I knew that this was how I got praise. I would never disrespect an adult, nor ever say "No".

After that night, life carried on, but this incident had a big impact on me. I probably developed quite a mistrust for men from then on. As my dad used to say, I had "a chip on your shoulder about men". After that, I would freeze if that uncle came near me. I didn't know what else to do. I simply froze. I remember another incident when he came into the house soon after I'd had my second daughter. My younger sister was sleeping in the front room. He entered the house, and I could hear him tickling my sister on her bed. I froze for quite a while, but then I cried out. He stopped touching her and came out of her room. He was a very creepy man.

I have no idea how much longer after that incident that the fire happened. That uncle lived interstate and he would occasionally "pop up" unexpectedly. I was terrified when I found out that there had been a fire at our house, in my parents' bedroom. I was especially horrified to hear that neighbours had seen my uncle hanging around our house shortly before the fire. Nobody was ever charged over the fire, but the impact on my mind as a child was that he had returned, as a warning to me not to tell anyone what had happened. He never touched me again, but there were times after that when her was around that I felt the same dread and fear.

I've since raised this issue with my family, although not with my Nonna Lidia, his mother. Apparently, while suffering poverty and hardship, an offer was made by the church to ease the burden by taking the eldest child to be "trained as an alter boy". He was, in fact, trained as a child soldier there. I have no doubt that he would have been sexually abused. He was just six or seven years old at the time. It's very hard to get anyone in the family to talk about this, but I know that, after that, Nonna turned against her religion, and that she would often say that priests could not put themselves in the place of God. Nonna also told us that we shouldn't wash the feet of priests or place them above us as they were people, just like us. Despite coming from a strong Catholic family, at some stage, Nonna decided to never go to church again.

I wouldn't want to hurt my grandmother, but on a couple of occasions she had wanted to talk about abuse in religious organisations with me. While she told me that she didn't see any abuse through the church herself, she understands that these things happen. To admit, however, that her own son had done anything like this would be devastating for her. I remain silent on this issue as she has suffered enough, and she is not responsible for her son's actions – only he is.

I believe that it is possible that this uncle sexually abused other female family members and female children of the single women he dated. I understand that airing these allegations is damaging, and that it hurts innocent people and that is not right, but he was not the only uncle in our family with this predisposition. Yet this was not the worst thing that happened to me as a child.

Chapter Two

On the Outside Looking In

We moved around a lot and changed schools often and various family members provided interim care while mum was unwell. When I was in primary school, we lived for a time in the country. I attended Nyamup, a tiny rural school with just thirty-seven children and, later, I went to Manjimup Primary where I made friends who I happily re-joined when I returned to attend Manjimup High.

Mum's illness never had a name to us children and, as was common in those days, we grew up with a sense of shame. Never was her illness discussed but, as a child, I overheard the word "crazy" many times over, always in whispered tones, as if this would somehow protect us children from the dangers.

Long, probing conversations with Nonna and Mum, in later life, revealed that Mum had her first "nervous breakdown" as a twelve-year-old, living in the refugee camps in Italy. Nonna spoke about the lack of food and their struggle to survive, but she also told me of my mother's amazing needlework skills, and how samples of her embroidery were taken by the church and apparently sent to the Vatican. Some topics from these discussions played on my mind, and I always wondered if child sexual abuse was part of that unspoken history.

I remember Mum's rages and her apparent "illnesses", her fears that she was going to die and days of her not moving off the sofa. I remember the arguments between my parents and, unusually for most children, I wished that they would separate and leave each other alone, instead of making each other so unhappy.

One memory is burned into my brain. I will never forget the tension before this happened, but I can recall little else about what had triggered it. While we were seated having our evening meal, Mum became incredibly angry. She picked up the broom and bashed it on the table. Screaming hysterically, she slammed the broom down, not more than six inches from where I sat. All of us sat there in silence, not moving, Dad at the head of the table. This snippet of memory sits alone, and I am unable to recall anything before or after. As if in testimony to my memory, I can recall the lemon Laminex tabletop and the three dents in it. I often used to sit near them and rub my fingers around the outside, as if to try and understand what they meant.

As time went on, Mum accessed mental health services both within the community and as an in-patient at the psychiatric hospital. Visiting these places was often traumatic for a child, but they also made me curious as to why people acted this way. *What was their story?* Then, of course, came the fear – the fear of their actions, or that I too could become like this. I saw their aggression, their pain, the loss in people's faces or conversations, and the way that, within this pain, connections were formed and friendships made.

Years later, when I visited the site of the hospital where Mum had often been committed, now the Heathcote Cultural Precinct, I realised that it sat amid the most beautiful parkland, at the top of a cliff, overlooking the Swan River. Although it would seem the most perfect setting for those needing to recover from mental health problems, I will always remember, as a child, questioning the decision to allow sick people such close access to those sheer cliffs that sat so high above the water. *Surely, many of them would choose to make that jump?*

Most of the buildings are gone, save one section, among the beautiful community parklands that the site has become. Recently, as I drove down to the entrance to the park, looking towards this building, I remembered an old man in his stripy pyjamas, masturbating, just as I had seen him on so many of my visits as a child. Funny what sticks in your mind and replays at the most unexpected times.

In those days, Mum regularly visited the community mental health service in Alma Street, Fremantle, and we children always tagged along. Often, these were short appointments to collect medication. As I recall, Valium was the standard drug given to women afflicted by the sort of emotional problems my mother suffered. One day, I remember her flying into a rage, pushing chairs around the waiting room in an attempt to get staff to provide her another prescription. We left hurriedly and travelled to her GP in Melville. A stern woman, Dr Simpson, knew and understood our family. Mum again grew angry, and I overheard that the clinic had refused to give her Valium, stating that she was addicted. Mum screamed and desperately tried to convince the doctor that this was not the case, but that she needed more. Dr Simpson, firm but kind, held her ground, and Mum became even more enraged. Again, my memory is lost, but I do remember waiting. I also remember an ambulance arriving and Mum being taken away. I remember arriving home, but I don't recall how we got there or who took care of us. And, I never remember anyone asking me if I was alright, or telling me what was wrong with my mother.

Back visiting at the hospital, the cold, sterile environment was punctuated by people shuffling about aimlessly, most of the time. The only exception was when meals were ready. Then, a sense or purposefulness took over and people smiled and greeted each other, as if they all had a common goal. The other bright spots I remember in hospital were the occupational therapy groups and the art projects that some patients were involved in. Treasured for years were the footstools Mum made for family members. These wooden frames with nylon or twine woven bases formed part of her physiotherapy. I still have one of those stools that my aunt gave me.

I don't remember how many times I visited the hospital or how many hospitalisations my mother endured, but I do remember, on two occasions arriving home from school and my mother not being there. We were never told what was happening and, if we asked, we were told she was in hospital. The tone of voice warned us not to ask any further questions. This response was consistent, regardless of which adult was currently caring for us.

I was born in the early 60s. Those were the days of children being seen and not heard. We, the children, were invisible both within the family and to all the mental health professionals. We had no voice. Nobody ever thought to talk to us, or ask how we felt, or to reassure us that it would be okay. As a child, you give time to your fears. This grief, loss, and secrecy was like an accelerant to my thoughts. I was not brave enough to ask questions or to make my voice heard, as I was still that "good girl".

When I turned eighteen, I was visiting Mum. I stepped outside to have a smoke when one of the nurses came out and began complaining about how difficult Mum was being. I was not offended as I had also come to this realisation many times, so, no shock there. This nurse, treating me as an adult, talked about the manipulation that my mother engaged in. Finally, I felt validated. Even within our family, we were unable to talk about this. The manipulation was an unspoken and most devastating effect of her illness. It created the perfect "crazy-making" scenario for kids who were trying to make sense of the world. At age eighteen, for the first time, I was able to ask what was wrong with Mum. Finally, I received at least one answer. The nurse told me that my mother had been diagnosed with "manic depression" – or, as they call it today, bi-polar mood disorder. It was many years later that I understood my mother's behaviour as attempts to have her needs met rather than outright manipulation.

Looking back, I can recognise the signs that led to this diagnosis – the frenetic activity, the wild spending sprees, handing money out in the street, giving all her belongings away, and not sleeping for days on end. Then there was the time the Federal Police contacted us, asking us to pick her up from the airport as she had been caught trying to board a plane to Argentina, without a ticket or visa. At that time, she was living with her mother. As her oldest and most responsible child, I was often called up at all hours to assist Nonna in dealing with the authorities because Mum's family struggled to manage complex communications in English.

I grew up feeling that the only time I got attention was when I did something that Mum could be proud of. Other times, I felt devastated by the lack of understanding or connection, as I struggled to parent my sisters while no one else helped.

One day, we were all playing outside and, as kids do, we were balancing on a 44-gallon drum, trying to walk or run on it. My younger sister was having a go and, as it barrelled towards the fence, she fell and became lodged fast between the drum and the fence. She got up screaming, and a trail of blood ran down the side of her head. My parents came running out of the house and started yelling at me for not looking after my sister better. I was always hearing, "You are the oldest! You are responsible!" I locked myself in the bathroom for hours while everyone went to the hospital to have my sister's head stitched up. Inside, I was screaming, *They are the adults! Why am I blamed for everything?*

Before the accident that would change all our lives, happier times with Mum revolved around her taking us to the Monument in Fremantle. It looked over Fremantle harbour, a short drive from our house. As kids, we rolled down the hills, getting up all itchy from the grass. Mum loved to dress us up and take photos of us there. Being girls, we also loved this time, and would happily pose for our pictures. It was my sisters who seemed to fit Mum's vision of the beautiful ones – both younger than me, the older of the two was tall and graceful, even as a child, and the youngest sported a cheeky little mop of bouncy, blonde curls.

On the Border

I didn't feel anger towards Mum for this – that came later, in my teen years. I didn't feel anything much, as Mum was a figure who drifted in and out of my life and consciousness. I guess, this was the beginning of me feeling that I was alone and could only rely on myself.

Chapter Three

Crash

We stumbled along in life, coping with mental illness, and extended family picked up the caregiving when Mum was hospitalised. None of us could have foreseen that life was about to get a whole lot worse.

On the 5th of August 1973, Mum had just been released from Heathcote Psychiatric Hospital again. She appeared a bit groggy when we left home where my Dad's mother, Nana Evie, was cooking and tending a beautiful, warm fire. As we were in the process of selling the Silas Street house to Uncle Emilio, Evie's partner, we were all living together.

We headed off in Mum's pride and joy, her red VW that Dad had bought her. Dad was driving and, on the ride home, Mum sat in the passenger seat, and my youngest sister sat in the backseat next to me. It was an overcast day, and it soon started to drizzle.

As we turned into Winterfold Road, Hilton, I rested my head against the little side window, feeling sleepy. The next period of my life is gone forever – perhaps, only visited in a dream-state when I wake up screaming – but it is something that will continue to terrorise me for the rest of my life. It was only a short time, maybe fifteen minutes or so, but my next memory is of standing knee-deep in mud, dazed, looking at the surrounding carnage. Mum lay under the other car. Someone grabbed me and, with strong arms, I was guided into a car where another woman sat next to me, screaming hysterically. I wanted to yell at her to shut up, but there were no words. It was like a bad movie that I could not understand.

I had a cut on my nose. Mum lay trapped under that stranger's car, and I was numb. I continued to feel like yelling at the woman to shut up, but I remained silent and stunned. The ambulances, sirens, rain, mud and shouting all muddled together in my head. On the stretcher in the back of an ambulance, I was raced off to hospital. In the corridors, which all appeared grey with not much light, I arrived at X-ray, passing another stretcher where my Dad reached out and asked desperately if I was alright.

That day, I was released and returned home to Nana's care. I had a broken collar bone and nose. Later, I found out that I had been thrown forward in the crash, and my shoulder had apparently snapped the gear stick and a few of my ribs were broken. My younger sister got a black eye. My parents sustained much more serious injuries. Dad stayed in hospital for a short time to undergo an operation to save his sight. From that day on, Dad forever saw double, apparently caused by damage to the part of the brain that controls sight.

Mum's injuries were life-threatening, and she teetered on the brink of death for many weeks. Lying in a coma, but reportedly often thrashing, screaming, and yelling obscenities to my father, she remained in hospital for about six or seven weeks.

The impact of the car accident was far-reaching and devastating. Life went on, but it was almost like it was in a vacuum. Another important turning point also occurred during this time, and this event further isolated me from my caregivers. We were a highly traumatised family with no support, other than family who didn't understand what was needed. My father, initially in a dazed state, almost set fire to his bed because, while smoking, he fell asleep. He has not shared with me exactly what occurred at hospital with Mum, but I do know that she would call out and verbally abuse him. Doctors had then encouraged Dad to say things back to her that would make her respond, and hopefully awaken her from her coma. I have often wondered what damage was done through this process.

My Year 5 teacher, Mr DeByl at East Fremantle, will always be remembered as someone who worked to keep me connected in those dark days after the car accident. I don't know if Mr DeByl is aware of the impact he had on my life, not only as a teacher. Daily, he asked me how my mum was. I would parrot off the latest information I had overheard, "Critical... Stable... Satisfactory". I would answer, but there was no feeling inside me. For a long time afterwards, I recall being alone and numb. However, this teacher's small actions served to ground me in the here and now. I worked hard at school, and Mr DeByl specially requested that I return to his class in the new year, as he felt that I had missed so much. I progressed to Year 6, but remained in his composite class. I am forever thankful for what Mr DeByl taught me but, more so, I am thankful for his compassion.

I hear teachers today say that they are not social workers, and that they should not have to deal with students' personal or family problems. I want to say that, as a teacher, you have the great chance and honour to make a huge difference in a young person's life. You may be the only person with whom that child has a voice. Later, I will share an example of an opportunity missed in my life.

Mum recovered from her coma, but sustained brain damage that affected one side of her body. Then began the long rehabilitation process. Transferred to Shenton Park Rehabilitation Hospital, Mum learned to walk, talk, and slowly coax her wasted muscles back to life. What courage and determination she showed in that twelve months! Her tenacity was truly amazing, and we often visited and celebrated her first few steps as she clung onto the parallel bars. Slowly, she began to feed herself and started taking care of her physical appearance again, something that had always been important to her. Later, she often bemoaned that she would never dance again, as she had when she was young but, for me, it was a miracle that she was alive and achieving milestones daily.

Of course, the mental health problems of the past did not disappear, but they seemed to abate for a time. Mostly, her mood was stable and happy, and the family planned for a future where she would return home and take up caring for us. As unrealistic as it seemed, this dream may have been the driving force behind her recovery. The harsh reality was to be much different.

Where the family had previously all pulled together to parent us, so began a period of conflict between our parents' families that saw an uncovering of barely hidden hostilities. Mum's mother, Nonna Lidia, lived in South Fremantle, and my memories of her home consist of a mixture of salty sea breezes and the sweet, tantalising smells emitting from the Arnott's Biscuit Factory where a lot of Nonna's friends, other migrant women, worked. Lidia was a strong woman who was used to making sacrifices and experiencing hardship. She worked hard, providing domestic services for well-to-do families in the Mosman Park area. Often, Nonna would be racing around, catching buses to work and back, after long hours of physical exertion, but she always found time to care for her family, especially her grandchildren.

Accusations flew about Dad trying to kill Mum, and these played on my mind for years afterwards. So strong was this conviction that, on the front steps of the hospital just days after he was released, Nonna attacked Dad with her shoe. After that, we children often overheard comments like "murderer" and "bastard".

During the time that Mum was in a coma, I came home and caught Dad being intimate with a neighbour. I was devastated, and I didn't speak to him for weeks afterwards. Nana Evie was living with us at the time, and we kids were all sleeping on the floor. Lying on the loungeroom floor, I heard Dad come in with the neighbour, a single parent who I knew quite well. Mum was in a position where we didn't know if she would live, and I felt tremendous anger towards my father for this affair.

I took out my full fury on Dad. I refused to talk to him, and lost all respect for him. He knew something was wrong and tried hard to talk to me about it, but I refused. I kept this up for about three weeks, ignoring any attempts to talk to me, or any directions he provided. In my mind, I was punishing him for his disloyalty and the hurt he'd caused me. I carried that lack of respect for him for a long time, and possibly it affected my view of all men. Later on, as I grew up and matured, I understood that sometimes the need for connection to others is important, especially when faced with trauma but, at the time, I was extremely angry and hurt.

My sisters and I had many caregivers over the years, and we even spent a short time in the Bridgewater Care and Assessment Centre for child wards of the State. I remember that we only visited there each day, while other kids lived there. The "house parents", I thought, were very cool and relaxed – so different to my homelife – with lots of laughter and teasing of the kids, instead of yelling. One young girl, probably a year or two older than me, often sat alone on a bench in the garden, looking sad. One day, I decided to talk to her. Bridget, as she told me her name was, was staying there because her mother had been killed. She asked me if I knew of Shirley Finn and, although I did not fully understand, I had heard that this woman had been shot in the head and found in her car. I recall feeling so sad for that girl, and I hoped that she would be happy in the future. But I also worried that she no longer had a Mum.

The mixture of violence and arrogance—shots to the head with no attempt to hide the body or strip it of valuable jewellery—indicated a professional hit. The facts present are that on June 23, 1975, the body of the flamboyant 24-year-old mother of three was found near Royal Perth Golf Club in South Perth.

Bridget, her youngest child, was the last known person to see her alive. A motive for the murder was never made known, which created a vacuum filled by rumour.

On the Border

(*http://www.crimenet.org/show_editorial.phtml?sid=ca6f9268460babf8ac da403fe34e19f1&id=796* Accessed 29 March, 2011. This link is not publicly available, but information about this event can be found by searching online for Shirley Finn. The murder was never solved.)

Year 6 for me saw major upheavals. We moved house, changed school, and I tried on many new roles. I remember arriving back home from school on the last day of the school year, skipping down the road towards the house, and excited at the prospect of holidays and Christmas. As I approached, I sensed something was wrong. I dropped the skipping and began to walk slower, taking in the scene before me. The car was packed up, overflowing with the last of our belongings, and the house stood empty of all things familiar. I was devastated. We were moving again, and I hadn't even had time to say goodbye to my friends. Still, no time for grieving.

We were moved to more suitable accommodation – a nice brick house in Spearwood, with no stairs, and easy access for Mum. She began to visit us. My favourite aunt, Dad's sister Rose, took care of us during this period, as my Uncle Gino was also in rehabilitation after a workplace accident. Aunty Rose is a beautiful lady who became like my mother figure, and taught me many domestic duties. This was a relatively happy time for me, as I liked the new school, and my cousins lived with us. Despite our rivalries, we had fun teasing each other about country versus city life.

Thankfully, the move to Spearwood Primary was seamless, and I settled in well and achieved excellent results. I was happy there. I had a good teacher, and even joined the netball club. Afternoons were spent with friends, chasing the ball around the court. I felt like I finally fitted in.

Third term brought another change, with our move to Hilton Primary. Academically, I was way ahead of others there, and this seemed to estrange me from the "cool girls" who were beautiful and resentful of anyone who garnered attention given to their achievements. So, I hung out with whoever was friendly to me. Oh, how I hated sports there! The teachers operated on the assumption that I was academic, so I must be sporty too. How wrong they were! I came last in every race I ran. Softball was double the agony for me as I have terrible hand-eye coordination, and I had to run as well.

During this time, I felt a burning ambition to use my abilities to become a social worker. This goal disgusted my father as he thought social workers were interfering "do-gooders". Rebellion rose within me, making this seem an even more attractive career. Over the years, I had heard how I would be "married and have a husband to look after me, so I didn't need an education". Little did Dad know that in saying that he only further fuelled the fire of feminism that would become important in my future.

Then, Mum and Dad picked out a house in Hilton Park to purchase as our new home. The large, weatherboard, ex-serviceman's house was similar to all the others on the street, which was dotted with housing commission homes. Standing on the front steps in Nicholas Crescent, I looked down the street to the park and had an unsettling feeling of desolation. It was the first time that I questioned my parents' decision-making, and I asked myself, *Why have they brought us here?* At twelve, no doubt I was on the cusp of adolescence and in for a rocky road.

South Fremantle High in the 70s, although modern, was less than a success for me, and I was constantly coming to the attention of our headmistress. It began with simple things, like uniform violations. I spent many hours outside of her office, missing classes. My appearances before that imposing headmistress Mrs Neville (later to become one of the first female principals, along with Ms Pow who was a dear principal from Manjimup High) became far too frequent and, try as I might to stay out of trouble, I always landed in the thick of it. I recall her telling me once that I was the "ringleader of all the troubled girls in the school". Boy, did I feel misunderstood! I didn't feel like a leader at all, just someone who was in the wrong place at the wrong time.

In maths class one day, an inappropriate drawing was being passed around. When one of my friends asked what was on the paper, I copied the drawing for her. Unfortunately, as I went back to completing my maths lesson, my artwork was seen by my teacher. I was sent to the headmistress. She made me write underneath the drawing, "This is what I spend my maths lesson doing", and asked that I get my dad to sign it. I was horrified. I could not bear to show my dad the drawing, so I drafted a new letter that stated that I had been caught smoking. He signed this, albeit with a grumble about wasting his time, but he was not that upset. Of course, I forged the signature onto the original note and my poor effort was not missed by the eagle eye of the trained headmistress. She told me that she would ring my father and talk to him. I replied that he was not home as he went away for work (he was a truck driver). Enraged further, Mrs Neville's face turned red, and she stated that she would talk to my mother.

"You can't," I said bravely.

"And why not?" the teacher demanded.

"Because she is in a psychiatric hospital."

Oh, I thought she was going to explode. "Get out of my sight!" she yelled.

I left, quietly relieved, but also wondering why she acted as if she didn't believe me.

I had initially wanted to be a paediatrician and, when I was fourteen, I saw the Guidance Officer to discuss this. He agreed that I certainly had the grades for this career, but suggested that I would need to put a little more effort into maths. He then proceeded to tell me that it would take me seven years of study after finishing school to achieve this goal. I was stunned. That was half of my life! It seemed so unachievable that I gave up my dream that day.

By the age of fifteen, I was growing increasingly difficult. One day, when Dad and I were fighting, in an attempt to hurt him, I yelled, "Yeah, well, you tried to kill Mum!"

Dad remained calm. He sat me down and told me that he had never wanted to hurt Mum and, even if he did, he would never take us children and put us in harm's way.

As was the way in our family, however, many secrets remained. It wasn't until many years later that the full story was told. Dad was a typical Aussie who didn't believe that the government should have the right to force people to use seatbelts. Our car fell into the category of not being required by law to have seatbelts. So, Dad, fatefully as it had turned out, removed the seatbelts from our car – a decision I am sure he will regret for the rest of his life.

Chapter Four

I Want to Learn a Love Song Full of Happy Things

She said, I want to learn a love song
Full of happy things,
She said, I want to learn a love song
Won't you let me hear you sing?
She said, I, I want to learn a love song
I want to hear you play,
She said, I, I want to learn a love song
Before you go away

For me, if there is a part of this story that indicates the impact of Borderline Personality Disorder and its personality traits most, it would be the unstable and unhealthy relationships that it causes. My need to escape from a family that was scattered and fragmented and with no sense of belonging, led me to seek love, without understanding what normal behaviour within relationships looked like. Added to this, was my unsettled life that made me vulnerable and naïve to the dangers that relationships could bring.

After months of physiotherapy, Mum came home to take over her role as wife and mother. But I was about thirteen by then, and us kids were pretty wild. Mum kept leaving and going to Nonna's place. Dad would return her but, in the end, Dad gave up as he learned that she couldn't cope with it all. It was unrealistic to expect that someone who had a brain injury, mental health issues, and children who were difficult to handle, could take all of this onboard without support. I guess that's how it was in those days.

On the Border

After our mother left, our father started a relationship with the woman neighbour. This woman was challenged with ending her own marriage while she and Dad entered their new relationship. Her husband lived in the same area, and I believe that he too was fighting demons, made worse by the loss of his marriage and family. One night, I was at home, tucked up in bed but not yet asleep in our lonely, empty house. I heard Dad arrive home and go to the shower. The phone rang.

It was late, and the shrill ring was a surprise. I felt a little concerned but, as I answered the call, the dread left me immediately. It was Dad's girlfriend. She spoke with a slight edge of urgency in her voice, and asked if Dad was there. I politely replied that he was in the shower. As I had never felt comfortable with their relationship, I put the phone down and went to the bathroom, knocking hard against the solid timber door. I could hear the shower running inside. Dad heard me, so I told him who was on the phone. Dad replied that he would be out in a minute. I casually returned to the telephone table, picked up the receiver, and repeated that Dad would be there in a minute. I went back to bed. As I drifted off to sleep, I again had a strange feeling. Perhaps it was her tone of voice or subtle speech, but it didn't stop me from closing my eyes and I was soon asleep, my head on the pillow.

The next morning began as usual, with no changes to the daily routine. I don't remember where my sisters where, but I do remember that, later that day, we were called to gather together. My father looked shaken, his skin pale and drawn. He told us that there had been an accident, and that his girlfriend's ex-partner had fallen down the stairs and died.

I hadn't been close to the man, but I knew him. I had wondered how he was coping with his relationship breakdown and with knowing that his wife had already re-partnered. I don't remember details, but I understand that this deeply religious man's body was returned to Scotland to be buried. His children were placed in care through the church, while their mother recovered from the loss. What stood out for me about this woman was that, although me and my sisters were quite young, it was made clear to us that she didn't want to parent us at all. I was twelve, and my sisters were just ten and eight years old, yet we were no longer a priority for either parent.

I no longer judge either Dad or his partner but, as a teenager, it filled me with rage that he could be with her when she rejected us so brutally. I hated them both, and this was the source of much recrimination against my father, well into my twenties. This animosity was only made worse when, by accident, I discovered that our Dad's girlfriend's husband had not died by falling down a set of steps. After that late-night phone call, Dad had entered his neighbour's house to find that he had suicided by hanging himself.

My own romantic partnerships began with this as a backdrop. The complex web of relationships within my family comprised firstly of our very ill mother who had returned to her mother Lidia's care, and secondly of our father who I believe felt a deep sense of responsibility to his new partner's children, now that they had lost their father. Still, with the naivety and optimism of youth, I believed that I could do better. I thought I would never make the mistakes my parents had made. This prophesy was, to a degree, workable for some time, but eventually I realised that I would make just as many mistakes, as I tried desperately to avoid repeating history.

My first relationship began at fifteen, in what was to be my final year of school. I met him over CB radio as, at that time, we had a live-in babysitter, only a few years older than me. Her boyfriend drove a big, yellow, F100 ute, and I often hung around talking on the CB while they chatted to each other. I remember being parked at the Pizza shop on the corner of South and Carrington Streets, a place where all teens hung out. We stood around listening to Queen blasting out of the car radios, "We are the champions. We are the champions... of the World".

On the Border

It turned out that I was the same grade at school as the sister of this guy I liked, Gerald. I remembered her from Year 7 at Hilton Primary School, although I had moved there for only the last trimester. Gerald and my relationship began quickly. I soon met his family and, from the outside, they seemed so close. There was always someone at home, which was so different to our place. In some ways, that family was what I thought I needed, so I threw myself in, boots and all. I knew Gerald had an ex-girlfriend and a baby daughter who he missed very much, but he didn't ever see them.

When Dad discovered that I was having a sexual relationship, he was horrified, and he immediately hated the person who had "taken advantage of his daughter". Although he was unhappy, Dad had to accept it, as he knew that if he did anything to my boyfriend, I was likely to leave the family altogether. By this time, another live-in housekeeper, a formidable Dutch woman, had moved in. Like most of those employed by my father to care for us, "Hans", as we called her, was on the lookout for a husband. I remember that some of these women were escaping dominating and aggressive men and, when Dad was not able to offer stability and security for them and their children, most returned to their abusive partners, due to a lack of options. Anyway, Hans was a wonder at running the household, and I loved this about her, as it was no longer my responsibility. When I think back, I remember her always leaning into Dad, especially when he had to fix the hot water system or attend to a leaking pipe in the bathroom.

One day, I had been in trouble for not completing some chores when I overheard Hans saying that she caught my boyfriend knocking at the back door the previous night. She told Dad that I had planned it, and had asked him to come over. I was outraged that she would lie like that and get me in trouble. If I had asked him, I would have owned up. When Dad confronted me, he didn't believe me. I remember standing in the laundry at the old wringer, feeding the clothes through the cracked, worn, rubber rollers, with tears streaming down my face. I felt a deep sense of sadness and I went numb. Then, an idea came to my head. I walked through the kitchen into the hallway and, just outside the bathroom, I found the large linen cupboard. On the shelf sat several bottles of mum's leftover medication. In a zombie-like state, I swallowed some pills and went to the kitchen to get a drink to help me swallow more. Casually, I returned to the washing and focused on the next load. Pushing them into the barrel-like machine, I watched them splash around and fed them through the rollers once again.

Dizzy and disorientated, I entered the kitchen and leaned against the walls to hold myself up. I stumbled down the hallway and knew I needed to get help. I called out for Dad. I remember making it to the front door before collapsing. I came to in the car as Dad was franticly speeding down High Street towards Fremantle Hospital.

He asked me what had happened.

"The tablets," I answered.

Dad accelerated as I passed out again, thinking that I would die and that he would crash the car. My only memory of that time in hospital was sitting in the window recess, looking out at the grey sky, and feeling sad that I hadn't died. I don't remember talking to anyone or anyone talking to me about what had happened. I felt like I was nothing. Dad detested the social worker, calling him a "cigar-smoking do-gooder", after he told Dad that he could not stop me from having this relationship with my boyfriend.

Somehow, life went on. I accept that I have gaps in my memory and that sometimes it may be better that I don't remember. My relationship with Gerald continued, but he was a troubled young man, and I wasn't old enough to understand him. He was a bit cheeky and a bit charming, and occasionally he broke the law. I was familiar with this concept, as it almost seemed a bit of sport among parts of our family to get the better of the authorities.

Aged sixteen, I gave birth to a beautiful daughter to Gerald, but within seven weeks things fell apart. We moved back to live with his parents so that, unbeknown to me, he could continue his relationship with his previous girlfriend. His father was a wonderful, kind man, a wharfie who had never raised a hand to his children. He was supportive of me, and promised that he would look out for me and his precious granddaughter. I don't think he knew what his son was doing. Sadly, I soon began to feel a strain in the relationship and, eventually, learnt the truth. Rather than being able to leave, if I raised the subject of Gerald's infidelity, I found myself the subject of physical attacks and verbal abuse. This violence always occurred when Gerald's dad was at work. His mother became my warden, reporting on what I did throughout the day, and ensuring that I was never favoured. The final straw came one morning, after my usual questions about where he was going, and his usual reply, "None of your business". On this occasion, I defiantly said, "You go and I'm leaving."

Suddenly, I was fending off massive punches to my head. I wrapped my arms around my face in an attempt to stop him hurting me, but he showed no mercy.

My degradation was complete as his mother stood in the hallway yelling, "Hit her again! She is nothing but a bitch!"

After the blows stopped, I threw myself on the bed and cried into my pillow.

He warned, "You better not leave the house, or I will kill you!"

As my bruised head throbbed in pain, I did not doubt him.

Holding my seven-month-old daughter, I stood at the bus stop around the corner from the house, trembling. I had a nappy stuffed down my shirt so I could change the baby if needed, and a few coins in my pocket. I had left the house with a warning from his mum to come back or I would be in trouble. I had agreed that I would return, and was just going to the corner shop. Despite the harsh sunshine reflecting off the road into my eyes and beating down on my skin, I stood shaking and shivering. I knew that if Gerald came back now, I would be subjected to another beating, and I was afraid that, this time, I would not survive.

Arriving in Fremantle, I found Child Welfare Services, who directed me to the back streets in the shadow of the Fremantle Prison where a refuge was located. They provided me with a cheque, as I had no money. There I was supported by the kind women, although I felt uncomfortable as most were much older, and no one was my age. I stayed for about four days, before I felt that I could leave safely.

I decided to leave the confines of the refuge, and walked into the centre of town to go shopping. Walking towards the police station, as that felt safer, I remained vigilant. It wasn't long before fast-paced steps ran towards me, growing louder and faster. I looked back over my shoulder and there was Gerald. I screamed, and began running towards the police station, but I was no match for his strength. Gerald grabbed me by the hair and pulled me back so that my head rested on his shoulder. Through gritted teeth he threatened that if I didn't give his daughter to him, he would kill me. Twisting my arm around behind my back, he turned me towards the refuge and propelled me forward. "Go and get her and bring her out."

Gerald marched me to the front door of the refuge, still pulling my hair and twisting my arm back.

I screamed, "Give him my daughter! Please, please!"

The staff remained calm and negotiated with Gerald. Stalling for time, they told him that if he let me come inside, they would give him my daughter.

Gerald knew that time was of the essence and that the police where in close proximity. I think this made him let me go. "I will get you eventually," he said.

I entered the refuge, sobbing and crying for them to follow through, or else I would be killed.

The staff calmed me down and explained that he didn't have the right to do this to me. After a time, I stopped shaking and was handed my beautiful baby girl.

I did, of course, get caught up in Gerald's promises that he would come back to me, and, at times, I became obsessed with what he was doing. It took at least another year before I was able to finally break away. I suffered more beatings and the regular nightmare of him coming to my home, assaulting me, and taking the baby. The police would be called, and they would always return her to me, but it was distressing.

One incident sticks in my mind, as I had friends staying with me who were from my hometown of Manjimup. We pulled into the bottle shop of the Hamilton Tavern, or "Hammi" as we called it. We were laughing and poking fun at each other when, suddenly, an arm came through the window and grabbed me by the throat. I struggled to breathe, and the driver leaned over, trying to make the man release his grip. My friend couldn't reach but, thankfully, he got out of the car with the intention of stopping my baby's father from strangling me. Gerald ran off, as my friend was easily twice his size.

The effect of this incident was profound, not just on me but on the other young woman he was involved with to whom he eventually had more children.

Over the years, Gerald continued to cause me distress and anguish. Not only would I hear stories about him fighting with his partner, including one night when he climbed into the roof and used a hammer to bash her in the head, but, months later, he also got into a relationship with my younger sister.

Growing up, I had heard rumours that the group of young men we associated with had made a pact to attempt to take the virginity of the younger sisters of their girlfriends. Gerald taunted my sister, telling her that he was with her to get back with me, and he sexually assaulted her by cutting her palms with scissors when she refused oral sex.

Aged thirteen, my younger sister began to show signs of mental illness. I was protective of her as, of all of us, she had been so young when neither of our parents had put her or her needs first.

One day, I was called up to my sister's school by the school nurse. I arrived, feeling intimidated. At seventeen, I carried my young baby in my arms. The nurse explained that the principal was concerned about my sister's health, and she wished to discuss it with me. The nurse acknowledged that I had not had a good time with the "said person" headmistress, but she assured me that she really cared about my sister. Part of me was thinking, *Thank God, someone is noticing that there is something wrong in my family*, but the other part of me held this image of this headmistress shaking her finger at me with my baby in my arms, and saying, "You turned out just as I thought you would". In the end, I could not face the headmistress. To this day, I regret that I could not make that step and overcome my own fear to help my sister who so desperately needed my support. But I also wonder, *Why was this complex problem placed on the shoulders of a seventeen year old?*

More painfully, years later, Gerald took on a large role in our daughter's life. Others thought that he was looking out for her through her pregnancy. I spoke to my daughter and acknowledged to her that, of course, I understood that she would want her father in her life, but that the man I knew "never did anything unless there was some gain for him". My daughter lost her baby, born pre-term and underdeveloped. Gerald visited her at the hospital and encouraged her to call me.

I knew that they had been working with the Indigenous family worker. Gerald had admitted that I was right to leave him, and that he would have killed me. But he also told the worker that he had changed.

My daughter laughed and giggled to me on the phone, saying, "Dad wants to talk to you." Gerald played coy.

Eventually, our daughter said, "Give me the phone. I will have to tell her… Dad said that he was wrong in what he did to you, and he is very sorry that he lost you, as you were the best girlfriend he ever had… He wants to know if you can get back together?"

I felt sick in the stomach. Firstly, at the thought of him trying to pull me back into a life I would never again enter, but more so because he had manipulated his own daughter in this way. Nauseated, I had to stay calm and polite, for my daughter's sake. Softly, I said, "I'm flattered, but my life is different now and I wouldn't want to change anything about how it is, as I am happy now."

Doing some work on myself again, something came up that I had purposely tried not to pay attention to when it happened very late last year.

Early December 2018, I received a group message from my eldest daughter's half-sister saying she had something important to say but would wait till a few others came online. Eventually she shared the news that Police had delivered to her just before daylight. Their father had collapsed on a railway platform and couldn't be saved, dying shortly after.

My immediate thoughts were to review my experiences of a very violent man who had not helped parenting his children and always blamed the mothers for keeping him away from him. Still my heart focused on the pain his sudden passing would cause his children. I thought about all the pain he had caused his partners and he was gone in such a mundane way, presumably from a heart attack.

I Want to Learn a Love Song Full of Happy Things

As I reflected over my early morning cuppa watching the news, I hear the breaking news stating a police investigation had begun after a male aged in his early sixties died at a train station. I felt my heart skip a few beats as my mind struggled to reconcile this news with the messages only 30 mins earlier.

Apparently, there had been an altercation in the car park and a woman and two men were wanted for questioning, as well as any persons who may have witnessed the events[1].

Along with the shock, my mind turned to thoughts of how that appeared a much more fitting death for a man who lived by violence and crime and had all the hallmarks of a true psychopath I found it really hard to feel sad about his passing and had a sense of Karma.

To his children I was compassionate and empathetic as I realised the full extent of their loss. Not only had they lost the physical presence, but they had lost any hope of him ever being the father they wanted or needed. To the adults around, I was able to share my true feelings and also sit with their starkly contrasting memories. From my daughter's stepmother, relief he was gone and anger at the trauma he had caused her, myself and others, to other family who remembered his cheekiness, sense of humour and charming nature.

I was so young when I met him, and the perfect victim, and I suffered for this trying to protect my daughter from that life. I wasn't successful, as it almost like the long-held secret and shame revisited the next generation and played out in her life in catastrophic ways.

---

[1] See newspaper article detailing this incident:
https://thewest.com.au/news/perth/victoria-park-train-station-reopens-after-mans-death-ng-b881038275z

Chapter Five

Loving in the Shadows

I met my first husband, Charlie, shortly after finally ending my first relationship. The only way that I was able to do this was by completely removing myself from my social group, a hard thing to do at seventeen. What had made it easier was a chance meeting with my next-door neighbour. We had lived in Hilton Park and went to school together, but were not close then. She was now married, and her and her partner loved children. We again became neighbours. They were a great help with my daughter, leaving me time to socialise and make new friends.

My husband was a reasonably patient man, and I would have to say that, during the first few months of our marriage, I was testing. I once was upset that he was late home. I waited until he arrived, and then set down his beautiful roast meal on the floor for the dog to eat. He was good with my daughter, having fun and playing with her.

We decided to get married, and were busy planning an April wedding, as well as the arrival of our daughter in October. We spent lots of time getting to know each other, and I found there were parts of his life that he found hard to share. Charlie had a very challenging childhood, and had been sent away from his family as an "uncontrollable child", spending time in Longmore and Hillston youth detention centres. His homelife was a chaotic blend of domestic violence, alcohol abuse, and poverty. He was one of eight children, seven boys and one girl, and had lost his youngest brother when he was eleven after an accident while playing cricket in the park.

He had been involved in more offending behaviour than he let on to me, and he was reluctant to speak about it. I found out that he had spent time in Fremantle Prison when he was younger, in his teens and early twenties. He never told me anything about it. I think perhaps that he didn't want it to change how I saw him or let it affect our lives – I found it hard to imagine my husband engaging in major crimes, as he generally was a jovial, calm man who liked dad jokes and played tricks for fun. He was attentive to others and most of the family loved and accepted him.

He did have trouble keeping a job, however, as I soon discovered. After he went through about four jobs in two months I began to worry. But he was always out there looking for another, and was rarely out of work. Eventually, my dad offered him a job driving trucks in his family business, and my husband never looked back – he loved it. He became well respected, and soon secured contracts for the business.

In the first few years of our relationship alcohol was an issue, as he came from a family of drinkers and it was a way of life for them. They were a very male-dominated family who all married women who seemed happy to serve their men. There were many large family gatherings where the women worked hard to prepare the food and ensure everyone's needs were met, while the men sat back and socialised and drank.

I never felt like I fit in with my husband's family. I was often in trouble from his mum who would say, "You are not a good wife", "Don't expect me to look after your kids", and, at family dinners, she'd proclaim loudly, "You shouldn't eat your dinner until your husband is happy. Make him his cup of tea now!"

I would reply, "Why? Are his legs broken?"

Many years later, I attended the *Charmaine Wilson Psychic Show*. Surprisingly, Charmaine chose me out of the audience for a reading. I was very emotional, listening to the other stories of loss, especially of young people lost to suicide. Charmaine asked me, "Why are you crying? I haven't even told you anything yet!" She went on to tell me that an older woman with a name starting with 'Fl', had died of cancer (and she gestured towards lower abdomen). She talked about this woman not being very nice to me, often critical. I was able to identify my mother-in-law who had long passed. Amazingly, she went on to say that, "She is very sorry. She was very unfair to you and she wants to let you know that you did well." I was so surprised that I got a reading and that, of all people, that woman was the *last* person I expected would reach out to me. Charmaine continued on about how she could see me ironing, and paused before asking, "Did you marry the favourite son?" We both laughed as I recalled that he had been, but that she had told him that he broke her heart. The further message from my mother-in-law was to my sister, "starting with S, ending in Y? Tell her I said hello," was the message. This was much more believable, as my sister had been in a relationship with the youngest son, and my mother-in-law didn't have the same reservations about her as she'd had about me.

I guess I was challenging to that family too, as I had very strong ideas and was not afraid to express my opinions. I also didn't like the amount of alcohol consumed at these parties as it often resulted in my husband being hungover the next day. I felt embarrassed too by his behaviour at times. I recall going to a wedding of a friend, and him drinking and loudly joking with everyone. I don't think that he offended anyone, but I still felt uneasy with his behaviour. I remember him having this habit of not being able to leave a party without a beer in his hand, and usually spilling it in the car as he passed out on the way home.

One particular time, I was really upset with him as I was five months pregnant. I had to try and get him from the car, up the stairs, and into the house. After about half an hour of having him leaning on me, instructing him to lift his feet to climb each stair, and guiding his full weight into the doorway, I dropped him on the lounge room floor. I was furious, and let go with a few well aimed kicks into his side. The next day, he woke up very sore and couldn't understand why. I didn't tell him until years later. He remembered the night well, as he experienced the pain the following morning.

My marriage gave me a sense of stability, and I was a stay-at-home mum most of the time, but did support the family business by shuttling drivers around, picking up parts, paying accounts, and doing general administration.

About a year after the birth of our son, I decided to return to study and fulfil my childhood dream of becoming a social worker. Looking back, my husband's resistance around my world expanding and not being satisfied with my life was like a forewarning.

Education remained an important part of my life and, as an adult, I made up for my teenage lack of appreciation for it. After having my three children, I knew that I needed something else in my life. I began a Diploma course in Social Sciences – Welfare Studies at the wonderful old campus of Perth TAFE. That feeling of success returned, and my self-image strengthened as I saw myself as something other than a wife and mother. Finally, I could become someone with her own opinions and thoughts (though, certainly not the thoughts and opinions connected to what I had learned in my family). I loved this period of personal growth that began in my late twenties, but I also found it confusing and challenging, in terms of all of my long-held beliefs.

During this period of educational and personal growth as an adult, the other major change in my life was that I began to feel that I was no longer loved by my husband. Whether this belief was real or perceived rejection, it was not an easy time for me, and I compensated by looking for that validation and affection elsewhere.

My husband was a good man, and didn't deserve what was to occur. To my knowledge, he was faithful to me, although he was a flirt and enjoyed playing up to other women. There was only one incident where he lied and left me waiting for him while he went out drinking with an old flame and returned home in the early hours of the morning. He admitted that he had enjoyed reliving memories of a younger and freer time, but assured me that no intimacy had occurred. I took this event really hard and planned to leave him, but my feelings of devastation led to depression, as my son was only a few months' old. I think that this time was the closest I ever came to a breakdown. I was unable to cope with what needed to be done if I had left.

Although I continued to function, this marked a messy time in my life. It was as if a deep, festering wound had opened up inside me. In my course, I had met a man who I was attracted to, and I also met up with an old female friend from my school days. Full of insecurity around my husband and her friendship and how easily they related to each other over a beer or two, I began to doubt that he really loved me. Maybe, in my own mind, this justified my next step. I commenced an ongoing affair over a number of years. Looking back, I was never in love with that man, but I did enjoy that he provided a sanctuary for me. When I was with him, I didn't have to do anything, and he cared for me. It was "time out" from my life that felt so stressful, especially as I coped with all of my family responsibilities alone. Apart from the children, I continued to support my sisters – one who had developed severe anxiety, and the other whose marriage had broken down nine months after her wedding and was pregnant.

When my husband found out about my affair, I tried really hard to reassure him that he had done nothing wrong. I took full responsibility for my actions, and tried to make him understand that it was me – that I needed a sense of closeness and intimacy and that he didn't trust me to share everything with him. My other big mistake was to open my marriage to a third person. I once read that girls without strong relationships with their mothers often connect with other girls with same experience, and that these relationships are unhealthy – that is what happened to me.

I did try to preserve my marriage and was creating space between myself and my female friend. She had left an abusive husband and became a big part of our family. When her son died, I remember watching my husband give her physical affection and comfort in such a beautiful way. I couldn't help thinking that I wouldn't be able to get her out of our lives now. *How could I after all that had happened?*

Eventually, the relationship with my lover did end but, as usual, I struggled to let go, both of my girlfriend and my lover. My husband and I endured a number of separations, and agreed that our home would be the constant for the children, so we alternated staying out of the home, in a shared care arrangement. Given this space, I was able to focus on my marriage and repair the damage, moving forward by setting some joint goals. What followed was a period of relative calmness for me. I still had to manage extreme behaviours from my son, but I took this mostly in my stride, only succumbing to short periods of exhaustion.

With a mortgage to pay, my husband gave up the family business for the security of a job in middle management for a small but growing transport company. He worked long hours and took calls all night, as truckdrivers wanted to chat when they arrived at their destinations. Suddenly, one day he went to work, and they gave him one month's pay and sacked him with no warning. At forty, my husband was crushed. He went to the Fair Work Tribunal and won his unfair dismissal claim, but was concerned about his future chances of getting employment in an industry where everyone knew each other.

We decided to travel for a few months, so rented out our house, and crossed the Nullarbor. Three days it took us, the second day marked with Jade and Jamie complaining bitterly about the length of the trip, so the fighting began. I stopped the car and told them that every time they fought, I would stop the car for 30 mins, and it would take forever to get to Queensland. Jade was defiant and jumped out of the car, stating that she was walking back. This only lasted a short time because she quickly stepped into a patch of 'double gees' and screamed, as she reluctantly realised that it was a futile exercise. We headed to Redcliffe in Queensland, as we knew that our friend would provide a good home base from which to travel up and down the east coast for what we hoped would be a three-month holiday.

We loved it in Redcliffe, Queensland, and my husband, always the workaholic, started to apply for jobs. A few months after arriving, however, we had to travel home to WA when my grandson died. On returning to Perth, I felt that I couldn't go back to living there, as there were too many traumatic memories, and I struggled to manage my family relationships. So, we settled into life in Queensland.

This was when I feel that my inherited traits of Borderline Personality Disorder became more apparent, and I feel that, in some ways, I was attempting to regain a lost childhood. Often, people sufferers of BPD are seen as aggressive and abusive, yet, conversely, we can also be incredibly vulnerable and naïve around how relationships work. I think that it mostly stems from our tendency to overreact emotionally. People often dismiss what I want to say because of my emotional delivery. I don't think that I'm a shouter. I just struggle with relationships and I think that a large part of that is based around my abandonment issues.

I must take responsibility for my own behaviour but, growing up amid such dysfunctional behaviour, you don't have a sense of what's right behaviour and what's wrong behaviour, so it took me many years to recognise the signs of abuse in men. Although I never suffered physical abuse again, I was married for seventeen years to my husband, and there was one time when he raised his hand to me. I packed up and took the kids and left. I left for a couple of days. He was very sorry, and he never ever did anything like that again to frighten me.

After my marriage broke up, I had what many would consider some quite unconventional relationships. For years, I lived on my own because I never wanted my daughter to be exposed to the fact that I did not choose the best men. I did, however, make the decision to become involved with a man who was already in a relationship. To me, this felt safe, because I knew where I stood all along and I couldn't face rejection. This was manageable within my lifestyle.

Managing my children's illnesses was not conducive to having a full-blown relationship as well. Any time I spent with my lover therefore became quality time; it was not mundane. I didn't have the time or energy to commit to more than that and, besides, *who would have accepted the things that I had to go through with my kids?*

My youngest daughter was the result of a casual relationship. He was single but, when he found out that I was pregnant, he disappeared. He moved to Darwin and left me to pay the load. Centrelink wouldn't pay me unless I made the effort to track him down, but he didn't want the responsibility. He admitted though that he always knew she was his daughter. He was very abusive as well, in front of our daughter, and there was an incident where he went to physically attack me and I had to lock the screen door. Then, his mum turned on me. She refused to talk to me. Before then, she had promised to pay for my flight back to Brisbane. She yelled, "It's always about money with you, isn't it!" She then refused to give me a lift to the airport. For many years after that, I had no further contact with them. She contacted me again, after he had two more children to two other women. She told me that he wanted a relationship with his daughter. I struggled with this as he is not a person I would want any relationship with, as he is not responsible. In the end, I relented for my daughter's sake, so that she has a sense of who she is.

Recently, he contacted our daughter. She wrote back and thanked him for contacting her, but explained that it was too hard to have contact with him because any contact she'd had with him had been quite devastating for her. Recently, her paternal grandparents visited her, and they thanked me for the wonderful young lady she is. They thanked me for how I've raised her. He has BDP traits as well, and I probably didn't recognise that until it was too late. He can turn on a dime and quickly become a monster. I've been happily married for two years now, and I value myself much more, but it's taken me fifty odd years to get here.

Chapter Six

Shifting Sands

Over the years, when meeting people in the community who had known Mum when she was younger, there were widely differing views of who she was. Some saw her as a beautiful, sweet innocent girl, while others remembered a disturbed young woman. The truth is, she was both of these things. On one hand, Mum was the much loved and a sheltered woman who was perhaps too innocent for this world. On the other hand, she was self-absorbed, irritable, aggressive and, at times, hell bent on ensuring her needs were met at all costs. I suspect she gained some insight when her favourite song became Alanis Morrisette's "I'm a bitch, I'm a lover, I'm a child, I'm a mother..." When I think about the biggest challenges of living with a parent with mental illness, two things that come to my mind. Firstly, the constant feeling that I was on the edge of becoming my mother and that I too would develop a mental illness. I recall a psychiatrist discussing this with me. He sharply announced, "Amanda, if you haven't developed a serious mental illness by now (aged 50), you're not going to." It was a relief to hear, but I struggled to believe it.

The second major challenge was that Mum's moods were not typical of Bi-Polar Mood Disorder. They changed very quickly. She could be very angry one minute, and then loving and charming the next. I later realised that this was about emotional dysregulation. The impact on us children, whether as learned behaviour or as inherent in our nature, was that we also struggled, at times, to manage our emotions.

As a parent, Mum loved us, but she was unable to provide us with support, either physically or emotionally. There were times when she relaxed and could be very loving, affectionate and attentive, while, at other times, I experienced her coldness and cruelty. Another big challenge that I felt was managing a lot of extra responsibility. Being the oldest, I felt this was my duty, especially looking after my sisters, but also, at times, caring for my mother.

One example of this sticks in my mind. I recall a particularly heated argument between my parents. Mum announced that she was leaving. As the eldest, I had the choice to come with her or stay with my father and my sisters. I was devastated that I had to make this choice. But, as quickly as I could think with my child's reasoning, I decided that if I went with Mum, I could make sure she was okay, and maybe she would come back. I went with her to Helen's Place, a restaurant near Fremantle Wharf that catered for many of the seaman away from home who were looking for a good meal. It was also my Nonna's workplace.

So, Mum, Nonna, and Helen, the restaurant's namesake, lamented over the happenings with the relationships, but without much reflection, the others continued to work hard serving customers. I sat alone with my head in my arms, leaning on the table for most of the night, wondering what would happen and if I would see my sisters again. Mum never spoke to me at all throughout her shift. When work was over, we returned home, still without any words between us. We approached the front door and, as Dad opened it, Mum pushed me through it, stating, "Amanda wouldn't stop crying, so I had to come back." My heart sank. I felt this overwhelming feeling of sorrow as I felt used. While I realised at about age eight or nine that our mother was mentally ill and that she would never fulfil what I needed in that role, my two sisters still wanted more from her. My sisters longed for the mother we didn't have until they reached their early thirties. They felt that she had suffered this horrific car accident and was therefore unable to take care of them from then on. I knew, however, that she had been incapable way before that. This process was shattering as my sisters committed to caring for Mum when Nonna decided to move to Queensland to live with her other daughter. Without the boundaries and behaviour management that Nonna had put in place over the years, my Mum's behaviour escalated very quickly. My sisters didn't have an understanding of her or what was needed to manage her. Mum's behaviour became visible in the community, as she would stay away from my sister's home, living on park benches and hanging around the coffee shops and cafes in Fremantle, often looking unkempt, and screaming. The situation was challenging for everyone, and I felt guilt around not caring for my mother, but, even if I returned to Perth, I knew that I would not be able to manage her behaviour. I decided I needed to give some support to the family, so I rented my home out and returned to WA. I hated every minute of it, but, when I arrived, I realised the full impact on my sisters' mental health in trying to care for Mum.

In 2002, Mental Health Services had decided to exclude Mum from any support, as she had been hospitalised a number of times and was aggressive towards other patients. They determined that she had Borderline Personality Disorder – an untreatable mental illness under the Mental Health Act. I was invited to a case conference set up by stakeholders who had been engaged with Mum, as they tried to determine how supports could be best managed. I was horrified as the reports by a psychiatrist stated that she had only one hospitalisation in a psychiatric facility, prior to the car accident. It is upsetting to be told that what happened when I was a child didn't really happen. Years later, I understand the need to draw the line in the sand, and that more resources were available for Borderline Personality Disorder that were organic in nature.

My Dad, although divorced for many years, still cared about what happened to Mum. He recognised that the family was suffering, and met with the Minister for Disabilities, Mr Paul Omodei. It was a pleasant meeting, as Mr Omedei had known Mum as he too had grown up in Manjimup, and empathised with the trauma that the family, and indeed my Mum, were experiencing.

On the Border

While waiting to return back to Queensland, I stayed with my sister and Mum for a short time. During that time, I had cups of coffee thrown at me, was hit over the head with a broom, and was called a slut and a whore in three different languages. I also had to deal with emergency services being called. Early one morning, I went for my usual exercise around 5:30 am. I arrived back at the house to find Mum calmer than when I left. I sat down to breakfast and heard a sharp knock at the front door. This was unusual, as we all used the back door to access the house. I walked down the darkened hallway and opened the door to two ambulance officers who stated that they were here in response to a call for help from someone who claimed she was being hurt. They said the woman caller had a slurred voice, so they were concerned she had experienced a stroke. I explained the situation and the recent meeting with hospital staff. Next thing, Mum runs up the hallway, holding her arm and dragging her leg, yelling, "Help me! They are hurting me!" The officer looked at me suspiciously. I stood there speechless. I turned to Mum and reassure her that she was okay and that no one was hurting her. At this, with the speed of a leopard, Mum turned and ran out the back door, leaving all of us stunned.

The officer became sympathetic, saying that they were concerned about her and should take her to hospital. I again let him know that mental health would not see her. They suggested a visit to outpatients, based on her claim to have a sore arm. They decided to try and find her and leave. Within about fifteen minutes, Mum returned and sat down, after making a cup of tea. Again, someone knocks at the door. The ambulance officer tells me how, as they were leaving, they received a call, stating that there was a woman lying in the middle of the road, a short drive away. They headed there, suspecting it was Mum. By the time they arrived, she had disappeared, so they returned to our house. I explained that she was back, and seemed calmer. The officers look concerned and, we agreed, that lots of attention and care might get her to co-operate, so they could take her to hospital. She responded well to this, and was happily placed on a stretcher. As they were packing up, the officers looked at my daughter Grace and said to me, "You know, she shouldn't be exposed to this." I nodded my head in agreement, and explained that I was returning to Queensland shortly. I felt lucky to leave this situation behind.

Fortunately, a Disability Package was granted to support Mum to live in the home that she owned. This was not terribly successful, however, as the home was not suitable as it was too large and on a sloping block with many stairs, and Mum's difficult behaviours led to workers not being able to continue to care for her for long periods. As she reached sixty years old, the government was able to provide her with aged care on the basis of mild dementia.

I was again called to take charge of a situation when, many years later, my sister Marie removed my Mum from the aged care facility and took her to Townsville, with little planning, medical records, or medication. Mum had been settled, and my sister didn't foresee that, without the structures around her, Mum would not be able to cope so well. Within three weeks, there was an incident where Mum grabbed a knife, threatening to stab her younger sister.

Townsville Hospital became my Mum's home for the next month, and only advocacy from a senior nurse prevented her being discharged to become a risk to the community. I had some discussion with the Social Worker around who could make guardianship decisions for Mum. At that time, my youngest sister was sole guardian. I felt again placed in the position of carrying the burden alone, but I eventually decided to apply to have an Adult Guardian appointed to make decisions regarding where Mum would live, who took care of her, and would be responsible for ensuring that all of her needs were meet. Mum was angry at me for my actions, and refused to talk to me. Although other family members, too, didn't like what was happening, it was agreed that it would allow the siblings to reduce the conflict that would invariably occur over the years, as decisions would need to be made about Mum's care.

I have the upmost respect for my both of my sisters for the care they have provided to Mum. I know that I am not up for the task, as I feel that to do so destabilises me. I don't think that my sisters are aware of the effects on themselves.

My youngest sister was suicidal when she visited me last year, struggling with so many issues. One day, she blurted out that our mother had turned on her when our other sister had decided to go to Argentina, in honour of Mum's wish to travel to her homeland. Mum had told her she hated her. As I had experienced many times before, it is almost as if Mum is not able to share any of her love with us all, and Marie was now out of favour.

Mum has never cared about the impact her moods, words and actions have had on anyone else. Even today, when I visit her, I find it very difficult and I have copped the most degrading, horrible verbal attacks. To add to the issues, the physical effects of that tragic car accident have made her paralysed down one side of her body. Having a relationship with Mum is like walking on shifting sands. One minute you're the favourite, and the next you're not.

Part Two
The Flower, the Lion, the Monkey, and the Gift

Chapter Seven

Parenting Prophesy

A very late honeymoon to Hong Kong in 1986 was the first time we had escaped from the family, our business, and our children. We arrived late that night, and I was fascinated by the city lights, activity, and huge crowds of people. It was a far cry from Perth's sleepy suburbs. This trip had been a long time coming as I had needed to convince my husband. He believed that he should explore Australia before heading overseas.

The children stayed with a dear friend who I knew loved them and where they would be looked after in the same way I would have cared for them. Our baby James was just ten months old, and I struggled to leave him, but I also knew that he was in good hands.

We did all the touristy things while there, and I shopped to within an inch of my life.

It was a steamy day when we headed over to the wharf, just as the sun was setting. An old man was looking for tourists to read their hands. He did palmistry and asked if I wanted my palm read. A tiny, thin, Asian man, he stared at me with really bright eyes that seemed out of place within his very old body. He clasped my hands in his bony fingers and gently turned my hands over to show my palms. He ran his fingers over the lines and gently muttered to himself. Finally, he told me that I had four children. I corrected him. I told him that I only had three. He looked into my eyes and laughed softly.

He told me about my children's personalities, describing the characteristics that he saw in each of them, without identifying their gender.

Firstly, he told me that my eldest was "beautiful, like a flower". He nodded and smiled again, "Fragile. Needs to be cared for gently, knowingly." He told me to appreciate her beauty, but to remember to care for her.

"Your second child," he continued, "is like lion. Strong, wise, and always hard to train." He warned me to be careful and said, "Watch how you treat them, or they will become wild. They want to be boss, like king of jungle."

"Third child. Oh!" and he laughed. "A monkey," he said. "Full of energy, hard to contain, always busy." He warned me to be careful as he would "tease you and make fun everywhere." The fortune teller became animated at the thought of the exploits my child may get up to. "But he will have a soft heart, this one, and will never want to leave his mum so you will also be trying to marry him off," he said.

My youngest child was born many years later, and, although not prophesised, I chose a name for her that reflects that she was a gift to me. She was unplanned, but raising her was a new and different experience, and one I did alone.

Chapter Eight

The Flower

My eldest child, Chantel, was born when I was sixteen. I was very young and involved in what was to become an extremely abusive relationship. Despite this, I took to the mothering role easily, and setting up a home was something I enjoyed. Thankfully, my Aunty Rose had taught me many household skills in the period that I had lived with her. After Chantel's birth, the hospital staff were trying to tell me how to bathe her. I felt insulted. I had been babysitting for years and loved children. The Matron was very strict and insisted that I give the baby up for adoption, but I held my ground.

I guess marriage and parenting was an idealistic fantasy for me due to my age. It was also a continuation of the nurturing that I was already undertaking for my sisters, though I am sure they felt it was more of a dictatorship.

Back to my flower. She was an easy baby to raise, contented and happy after the early weeks of colic and lactose issues. As she reached seven weeks of age, however, our life took a turn. Gerald decided that living and working in a small mill town in the south-west of WA was not for him, so we moved back to Perth to live with his parents.

My relationship with Gerald deteriorated and, eventually, the violence resulted in me escaping with her to that refuge. I am forever thankful to the staff of that centre who protected me, and advised me that he couldn't do this to me.

Unfortunately, the end of that relationship was drawn out and messy, involving ongoing abuse. He made allegations to child welfare. Thankfully, the government officers understood the dynamics of domestic violence. I was offered respite, and for a week my daughter was placed in Ngala, a service that supports parents, families and communities. I missed her so much that I travelled to pick her up after a few days. I realised that the only way I could truly be free of him was to move away from this community and build a new support network. Years later, this resulted in much criticism and blame for my daughter's emotional and spiritual issues, as she was Aboriginal. However, it was not safe for me or her to maintain a connection with her father at that point. At least, as a 17-year-old with a young baby and limited support, I didn't know how I could do it.

My Flower truly was a beautiful and happy child. She made friends wherever we went and, although not academic, she loved engaging in school and Sunday school. She played sports, and she loved her family, especially her younger brother. Her little sister always complained that, when *her* friends came over, they were attracted to Flower and her bubbly personality.

I recall one day when I was called to the school about her. I was shocked. As I waited for the principal to see me, I remembered all of my own awful times, sitting outside the headmistress's office at school. When I was called in, I realised that I was not in there due to my girl's poor behaviour, but rather to receive an apology. Apparently, she had been sent out of class, not because she had done anything wrong; rather her teacher had a breakdown and was suffering PTSD. He had to leave the school and they were busy talking to all of the parents about what had happened, as the children had been surprised by his behaviour.

When Flower reached Grade 7, teachers identified that she was struggling with maths. Everyone agreed that her compliant nature had led to teachers overlooking her lack of understanding of maths in her earlier years.

The impact of trauma on Flower was not immediate, and she appeared to be coping. Looking back, I can remember no issues with her behaviour until she went through puberty. As we engaged with support for her brother, however, she asked if she could talk to his psychiatrist too. The doctor's feedback to me was that she was a very articulate young girl who knew what she wanted. She was struggling with the fact that she had been cruel to my friend's son who had died recently, and she felt guilty. The psychiatrist reassured her that all kids say things they don't mean, and that it didn't relate to him dying.

The onset of puberty saw massive changes in Flower's personality. I always describe it like someone "beamed my daughter up and replaced her with a complete stranger". I struggled to maintain my connection to her, and I didn't understand what was going on. Within a period of three months, she was stealing, truanting, running away, promiscuous and angry. Twice she was found passed out after "chroming" (a form of volatile substance abuse involving inhaling solvents or other household chemicals), and despite me attending the hospital she refused to come home.

From an early age, Chantel had always talked about seeing spirits, and this spiritual side of her life was not something I understood. Some kids have imaginary friends, so I just shrugged it aside. When I was raising her, I just accepted her for whatever she said or did. Even today, I wonder if this was the earliest manifestation of mental illness or, as she has described it, whether it is part of her Indigenous connection.

By the time Flower was thirteen, I had no control. She did return home, and, for a short while, I thought everything might be okay. But that all ended one day when she stole a large amount of money, went to the city, bought a dog, and got piercings. She returned home and smashed the window of the house because the door was locked, as no one was home.

Seeking support, I contacted a number of services, Child Welfare being first. As I had been a foster parent, I knew that they may be able to help me get appropriate care. They did their usual assessment, and stated that they didn't believe there was any abuse of her. The worker suggested that perhaps it was just a stage and that, "One day, you will look back and laugh at all this."

Meanwhile, Flower was living with a heroin addict a few streets away. One outreach service went to visit her. They told me that she was a lovely girl and not to worry too much about her. They also said that she loved me very much and appreciated the cards and letters I sent her, in which I kept telling her how I loved her and missed her. But I was never able to break through.

Eventually, Flower teamed up with a boy who was to become the father of her children. She moved in with his family and, for her, it felt right to have found her cultural connections – something I was not able to give her.

Initially, I was told that it was my daughter's lack of connection to her Aboriginal culture that was the issue, not any mental illness. I felt so much guilt about this, and also that we moved to Queensland without her, as she refused to come. The outcome was tragic. Chantel became the victim of devastating and traumatic domestic violence, losing all of her children to the child protection agency. I am so frustrated that our family history was ignored in favour of her Indigenous heritage, and that my grandchildren not only suffered foster care, but also that nobody foresaw or validated our family history of Borderline Personality Disorder.

Chapter Nine

The Lion

My second child, Jade the Lion, was born two years later and was totally different from the start. Arriving after a long and tiring labour, which culminated in Charlie insisting that she must be a boy; the doctor disputed this, and the room grew so heated that I was worried they would come to blows. Strangely, I did not have the same confidence in handling her as I'd had with my first. Despite her being planned and very much wanted, I didn't feel the bravado I had previously felt.

At Woodside Maternity Hospital, I shared a room with a lady who rejected her baby. Refusing to have anything to do with him, she threw the flowers that her husband had bought her back in his face. I didn't feel like I didn't want my child, I just wasn't confident that I could care for her. My husband made the situation even worse when he bought in a magazine article about choosing the sex of your child. This triggered memories of when my mother insisted that my father wanted a son, and was disappointed at having us three girls. I felt that I had failed, and history was repeating itself.

I had a dear friend who, despite us trying to conceive at the same time, remained childless. She had been a great support to me during the previous year and she continued to provide a role model for me in how to develop attachment to my children. I am forever grateful for her support throughout my children's development.

As a toddler, Lion experienced regular night terrors. I took her to the antenatal nurse who told me that this was normal. Lion would also bite her cousin every time she saw him. "You can come around for coffee, but don't bring her," my sister warned me.

Isolation and emotional exhaustion led me into "extreme parenting".

As a small child, Jade threw many tantrums. She loved to hide in very small places, like cupboards and boxes, and developed a foul mouth when things did not go her way. My Lion struggled to get on with other children, and parents often shunned us due to her behaviour. Parenting her became stressful for me at times, as I didn't have the skills to manage her challenging outbursts. On reflection, I didn't understand attachment parenting and certainly lacked experience in how to deal with her. As a consequence, I began to distance myself from her at the times when she most needed me to help her regulate her feelings.

Beautiful, brave child that she was – and super intelligent – she went on to enter the Gifted programs throughout her schooling. I was often at the school helping out, especially typing up the stories for the children on the large typewriter. One day, I was tucked away in the side room of the junior cluster when the Grade 2 teacher came to see me. She asked me what my husband was like. I replied that he was quiet. She said, "You are too, so how did you get a daughter like her?" She went on to say that Lion was very intelligent, "but not as intelligent as she thinks she is." She continued, "She is lacking in any imagination and, at times, empathy."

We followed this teacher's suggestion and went to see a psychiatrist. The doctor reassured me that Lion was fine, and only needed a firm hand as she was strong willed. In fact, he stated that I should "smack her" as the pain would interrupt her thoughts, as, he said, "She doesn't have any window of opportunity to break her own thoughts."

So, after that, I used to hit her. It hurt my hand so much that I then used a belt. A few years later, she ended up burning it. She and I laugh about it now. She threw it in a fire one evening. In hindsight, my kids never encountered a lot of physical discipline, but I don't believe the hitting helped.

Jade wasn't cruel, she just struggled at times to see others' point of view. As I look back, I wonder if she had autistic traits. She couldn't stand too much noise and would often place her hands over her ears.

Learning came naturally to my Lion, and she loved Sunday school. She delighted the staff at the Salvation Army in Hamilton Hill, as she could memorise the bible. I supported my children being involved in the church. Although I didn't have any strong beliefs, I somehow felt that I would need help in teaching my kids good values.

Jade gave everything a go and excelled at most things. She was tough, however, and often seemed insensitive to her own feelings and those of others. At home, she liked to have control and we sometimes butted heads. She felt she didn't see herself as a child, but rather as my equal. She liked order, and this state became increasingly difficult to maintain as her brother grew older.

In high school, Jade attended an academic excellence program, not in our local area. She found it difficult to get on with her peers. She was bullied badly, and the school suggested that going back to her local school would be best for her. So, she moved schools and felt happier, being together with the kids she had gone to primary school with.

When we moved to Queensland in 1995, Lion was devastated. Despite preparing her and her agreeing to the adventure of travel, for years afterwards she blamed me for ruining her life. So began her drinking, truanting, and the ramping up of defiant behaviours.

Unlike Chantel, Jade remained at home until she turned fifteen. She then lived independently, but returned home regularly, enabling me to maintain my relationship with her throughout what were to be turbulent years. I had refused to continue to go to school for re-entry interviews, so she left and gained a traineeship in pharmacy, an area in which she has excelled.

This traineeship was a very positive move for Jade, and she excelled in her practical work and in gaining her certificates to become a Dispensary Technician. She became a mother, surprising me on my fortieth birthday with news of her pregnancy.

The baby's father had his own issues, and he subsequently began another relationship, getting a second woman pregnant. This destabilised Jade further. On the outside she looked very successful, but she had begun gambling and self-medicating with alcohol. Eventually, she had to seek bankruptcy. Jade is a very hard worker and repaid all of her debts, but continued to struggle with addictions.

Jade moved to the wonderful Whitsundays for a new start, and secured a job as retail manager at a large pharmacy near Airlie Beach. Grace and I visited her there often, spending many magical holidays visiting Hamilton Island, Whitehaven Beach, and other tourist attractions in the area.

Sadly, addiction was an ongoing issue for her, as were relationship issues. She fell pregnant to a man who was not interested in a relationship at all. This abandonment saw Jade's life spiral out of control, and her vulnerability led to her marrying a man who she thought would provide her with stability and security, but nothing could have been further from the truth.

Jade's husband was a compulsive liar, controlling, and enmeshed with his family. Jade wasn't able to actively make decisions in her own best interests or for her children, so this started a period of decline in her mental health. Eventually, she was admitted to a mental health unit and detox unit with the diagnosis of Borderline Personality Disorder (BPD). She lost custody of her two youngest children. I had to make the hard decision to stop supporting Jade, and focus on caring for her oldest child.

Medications were fairly ineffective in treating BPD. Jade's faith, strengthened by Rehab with the Salvation Army, is what gets her through those tough times.

Through family court she underwent two assessments both agreeing that she showed no signs of BPD or alcoholism and that she was unlikely to relapse unless she experienced long periods of extreme stress.

I am grateful to still have her and am amazed how her faith enabled ongoing education and employment working with families.

Chapter Ten

The Monkey

My boy was born after a long and tiring pregnancy and labour where I was told the baby was distressed. He weighed 10lb 2 oz and arrived fist first to the exclamations of the nurse, "He is a monster!" He was beautifully plump, aware, and as big as a three-month-old baby. Charles was ecstatic to have his son.

Exhausted, I was left alone with him in the darkened room, barely able to lift my arms to cuddle him. I had the name Daniel picked out for months, and had convinced Charlie to let me call him that, but, as he lay on my chest that morning, I explored his round little face and soft downy blonde hair, and decided he was "James". Charlie, in his excitement at having a boy, didn't mind what he was called.

He was so loved and indulged by his sisters, and was never short of someone to watch over him or give him hugs. I persisted with breast feeding for four months, but he appeared to not be putting on weight. He was very active and, like the others, a bit fussy, as well as lactose intolerant. Unlike the others, Jamie wouldn't drink soy milk, so I had to find a health food shop that stocked fresh goat's milk.

Like most monkeys, Jamie was forever on the go, and I was surprised that before Christmas in 1985, at less than four months old, he had army crawled across the room, making a beeline to the presents under the tree. He was happily sucking on the brightly coloured Christmas wrapping paper. The girls and I had a great laugh as I picked him up and washed his face that was covered in green and red dye.

The other special relationship James had was with my Nonna. She would sit for hours with Jamie across her lap, gently rubbing his back and patting his nappy. They had an amazing bond and, on Sundays when the family met for lunch, I could always be happy, knowing that Nonna and Jamie loved the easy peacefulness of time together, both in their element.

Off and running at ten months old, Jamie was a ball of energy. It was a true predictor that he would always be up to something. He loved attention and climbed everything, making it a constant job to contain him.

Looking back, there was the beginning of what I now realise where sensory issues. He sucked his thumb, he developed a preference for a certain blanket on his cot, and he had aversions to certain things. In 1986, the alien character "ALF" was big on TV. Every time that Jamie saw it advertised, or the girls wanted to watch it, Jamie would become hysterical, climbing up his dad's shoulders and wrapping himself around his dad's neck, then peeking out to check if ALF was gone.

We worked really hard to desensitise Jamie to ALF and, by his first birthday, we had won. He loved the ALF stuffed toy we bought him, and would carefully tuck him into his bed at night. The aversion to anything unusual, such as clowns, Humphrey Bear, and even Fat Cat remained, however, making it hard to engage in community events that other children enjoyed.

Jamie loved his dad and followed him everywhere when he was home. Their favourite game involved Jamie pretending to hit his dad who would then fall to the floor, feigning injury. We would all look concerned, and ask if we should call the ambulance. Jamie would look so upset and would rub his dad's face, shaking his head to rouse him. Jamie's little face screwed up with concern, showing empathy, as only little ones can. Suddenly, his dad would come back to life and they would both laugh together, with Jamie looking proud with a beaming smile because he had saved him.

The Monkey

In true monkey mode, by eighteen months, Jamie had mastered opening our latched windows. Two feet from the ground, Jamie hoisted himself onto the frame and swung his legs up and over to slide down to the concrete on the other side. This was his favourite trick when he wanted to see his sisters who were at school, just a street away. I would chase him, and he would laugh as he ran faster to get away from me. So, he became my cheeky monkey.

In 1988, we travelled as a family to Bali for Christmas.

At age four, Jamie was enrolled in a kindergarten program, but he wouldn't leave me. He clung onto my dress and hid behind my skirts. I didn't have the heart to make him stay so, after a few days of trying, I decided I would keep him with me another year.

The next year, Jamie attended a fulltime pre-primary program while I was studying. Enrolled at a private Catholic College, he commenced his education. The staff where so kind to him. They patiently protected his self-esteem and never made any negative comments about him, only letting me know that he "wasn't naughty", he just had some "odd behaviours", like standing at the toilet and watching his lunch being flushed down it, not eating, and not staying in prescribed areas.

1990 saw his first year at big school and the only year that Jamie attended the same school as both of his sisters at the local state primary school. As with the other children, I volunteered in class support. I was perplexed by what I saw. Jamie rarely sat in his seat, was standing on desk, and ate pencils and his glue. I couldn't understand why he behaved like that and, secondly, why the teacher didn't talk to me about it. I thought that, perhaps, it was because I was in the class. So, I arranged to do other work at the school that wasn't classroom-based.

At the end of first term, I received Jamie's report, requesting a meeting with the principal. Struggling with his behaviour at home too, I didn't know what

I was going to say that might be helpful. The Principal was very kind and understanding. He talked about having extra support for the fraught teacher.

After the holiday break, the return to school came quickly and, with it, an event that would change the course of everyone's life.

Chapter Eleven

The Gift

My Gift, Grace, was born just as Jamie was entering his most difficult adolescent years. I feared greatly that I would have another child with challenges and, again, would not be able to manage.

The unplanned pregnancy was easy, and I had accepted that I would be alone in parenting her. When told of the pregnancy, her father didn't look shocked, but replied, "Oh, I didn't think I could have kids as my ex-girlfriend and I had tried for years and it hadn't happened." He had no interest in becoming a father, and I knew that I would have to manage without him. He did, however, offer to help in any way if I let him know. He quickly disappeared interstate and left no forwarding address.

Luckily, I had a great support network at the time, and was heavily involved in community work in the area of Domestic Violence. So many beautiful women checked in on me, gave me emotional support, and even arrived with some rib eye fillet, "to keep the iron levels up". I also had some male friends supporting me during the pregnancy and after the birth, who provided company, car repairs, and the occasional cooked meal.

I had considered and planned for adoption in NSW, due to adoption laws in Queensland that restricted open adoption. I was very determined that this was the best way to proceed. In weekly contact with an adoption counsellor, I had my train ticket and accommodation booked when I arrived in Sydney. Not only did I carry the fear of having another child with behavioural issues, I also had so many worries about the paternity of the child, but I refused to be defined by that, and was open to accepting that I had made a mistake, and that my feelings about my child may be affected by who the father was.

My plans fell in a heap when, at thirty-six weeks, I was told I needed to proceed to the maternity ward immediately, as my baby was a transverse lie, and my life and that of my baby could be at immediate risk. I was not even allowed to go home and get clothes. I protested, but they held firm, and I sometimes wonder if they didn't stage their own intervention to prevent the adoption.

Grace was born on a Friday night, and my friends and I enjoyed music, chips, chocolates and coke while the labour was induced. It went quickly and easily, and, in the early hours of Saturday morning, I gave birth to my beautiful, petite, baby girl. My support women rushed home to get Jamie, and he was one of the first people to hold her, beginning the bond that would sustain her throughout her early years and into adolescence.

Two days later, I had a long conversation with the adoption counsellor who offered to plan to have the adoption proceed by arranging an emergency carer come to get Grace. I didn't hesitate to say I wouldn't be needing that, as I literally had fallen in love with my daughter. None of the issues I had worried about prior to her birth mattered. I knew I would be okay.

Grace was a pleasure to raise and, without the complexity of the other children's behaviour, she was a breeze, at least until she reached her teenage years. A princess, Grace loved attention and, as the older siblings were there, someone was always around for her. I remember that she would often stand on the coffee table as a toddler, and just free fall off, knowing that Jamie, myself, or Jade would be there to catch her.

Grace went to day care from about six months old, and was loved by staff there. As a young child, she had many friends and was often invited to parties or activities with friends.

The Gift

Grace and I travelled at lot together, and we developed a very strong bond. She didn't seem to miss having a dad around, as she still had family that were close and protective of her. She did meet her dad's family when she was young and, despite her unconditional acceptance of everyone, she felt the need to protect me from her father. I did not want to put her in that position, and so I decided that seeing her dad could wait until she was much older.

As protective as I was of Grace, I wasn't able to fully shield her from the worst of Jamie's behaviour. Jamie was thirteen when she was born, and he was already using pot regularly. There was an incident when she was three months old. Jamie was drying pot in the microwave, and the house was full of fumes. I was furious, and concerned for Grace. I ended up telling Jamie that he could no longer live with us. He went to his dad's for a short time, and this led to the only investigation by Child Protection. They determined that I was emotionally abusive to Jamie. *How do you deal with impossible choices, and what other options are there but to raise your children the best you can?*

Grace was very possessive of me, and didn't like to share me with anyone other than her siblings, so my relationships were difficult, and I learned to manage them outside of my time with her. Any males she was exposed to would have seemed like friends.

The first relationship that Grace would have recognised was when she was about seven. She did not welcome the intrusion on our lives. She loudly complained the first night that "I don't want to share my Mummy", along with crying and screaming that we had to return home.

Eventually, Grace came around and enjoyed it, as mine and my partner's families came together, at least initially. At times, Grace began to develop anxiety, so I quickly got her some counselling, but it would come up, from time to time. Looking back, bullying from my stepdaughter impacted Grace, combined with unhealthy dynamics in the family that I didn't realise at the time.

The end of that relationship was stressful, and the disclosure of sexually inappropriate behaviour by my ex towards Grace rocked our world severely. After the police report that we knew wouldn't result in a conviction, I arranged counselling. We went through so much together that I can say that, after the first six months of leaving, we were both in a robot-like state. Grace slept, clinging to me every night, alternated between hating him and begging me to go back to him, as she missed our old life.

When we finally sold the house and completed the settlement, about a year later, Grace and I moved into a new home, complete with granny flat for Jamie. Two weeks later, we flew to the USA for seventeen days, on the trip of a lifetime.

An incident in Las Vegas, however, left me reeling. Following a show at The Luxor, Grace and I had a minor argument, right near the end of the Strip. We were leaving the hotel, and she was yelling at me. I said, "I am not arguing Grace. We are going back to the hotel now", and I headed to the bus stop across the road. While waiting at the lights to cross, I turned around and she was gone. I nearly collapsed. I didn't know what to do, or who to go to for help, and I was terrified that she had been kidnapped. I ran back into the casino and asked them to call her on the loudspeaker. After I told her that my daughter and I had had a fight, the woman looked at me like I was an abuser.

The woman on the phone was much more reasonable, and told me she would announce Grace's name, hoping she was still in the hotel. I stayed online for five minutes, panicking that, if she was kidnapped, I was wasting time in the casino trying to find her. "No luck," said the lady, and asked me to go back to the original desk where I had sought help. The lady was even ruder this time, ignoring me completely. Finally, someone noticed my distress. The security guy was sympathetic and, comforting me, he asked me to accompany him to the security office, as I begged him to get the police. I spoke to police, and we worked out that it was best to go back to our hotel and hope that she had returned, but they warned me that Vegas is the capital of sex slavery and child exploitation. On the upside, they said that, due to children's curfew, she would be very easy to stop if she was on the Strip.

I was beside myself as I caught a taxi back to our hotel. I asked to see the security there. I very tall and stern man responded to the desk's phone call, and approached me within a few minutes. Instead of a friendly approach, I was taken aback by his monotone voice, stating that he had jurisdiction over the hotel and, using this power, had entered my room and searched it. He noted that it was very hot (we had left air con on), but he could not locate the child. He also advised that he would accompany me back into the room, which was being guarded, and that we would search together. I felt like a criminal, and was worried that I would be arrested, together with Grace.

As I entered the room, he received a call from the security office and told me that she had been located. Grace was now detained in the security office of the hotel as she had attempted to get a room swipe, and she was under 18. I thought to myself, *We are in way over our heads and I don't know what to do*. In the hallway, a very large African-American police officer met me in the hallway and instructed me to sit in the small office. He said he would speak to me shortly. I was scared, as he was well over six-foot-tall, with shoulders like a wrestler.

I waited alone in the room while he interviewed Grace and, although I was relieved that she was safe, I still worried how this might turn out.

Eventually, his commanding presence entered the room and he said, "So, you had a fight, eh?"

I nodded my head and quietly said, "Yes".

The officer says, "Does this happen often?"

I responded, "Not a lot, but she is a teenager."

With no let up from his serious tone, I begin to think I'm in big trouble. Next, he asks, "Do you hit her?"

I crack at the absurdity of this, saying, "Would you? I mean, you've seen her!"

Finally, he smiles. "She gets pretty angry. You would think that walking the Strip would have calmed her down, but she is still fiery."

We laughed together, co-conspirators now trying to rein in a wild child. He told me to stay in his office while he had a stern talk with her. A few minutes later, I went in to see Grace.

As I entered the room next door, my daughter was still furious with me. The officer advises that we can go back to the room, but only under escort of security. I try to talk to Grace about how dangerous what she did was, and she shrugs me off. On the way out the door, Grace pushes me with her shoulder.

"Stop!" yells the police officer.

Grace and I jump at the force of his voice.

"Don't you ever disrespect your mother like that again. Do you hear me, young girl? I have wasted the last few hours looking out for you when there could be serious things happening, and this is how you behave?"

Grace nodded her head, after a few seconds, not really wanting to give in, but also not sure how serious he was.

We walked away in silence as the security guard returned us to our room, through the casino, with all eyes on us. The guard dismisses the officer at our door, and leaves us alone. Grace removes her new boots, beautiful suede boots with a frill around the top and spikey heels that must have been so painful. I giggle inside at the thought of her not noticing this, as she is in such as rage. She looks at me like a very sad child, and my heart melts.

"Please don't tell anyone what happened," Grace pleads.

I nod my head in agreement, knowing that this story will create some laughs in the future, but for now she needs a big hug.

From that time on, Grace began having trouble regulating her emotions, even positive ones. When upset, she became so distressed she would attempt suicide or self-harm. Grace's first overdose resulted in the police taking her to hospital under an Emergency Examination Order (EEO) for assessment. Another time, she cut huge chunks out of her beautiful long hair.

We began counselling, and they indicated to me that it was very likely that she had Borderline Personality Disorder but, until she reached eighteen, they would not diagnose this. They acknowledged to me that I probably knew more than they did about this disorder, and that I was doing all the right things. I agreed that I could handle it this time, but I thought I should give Grace the option of seeking support. The other important revelation then was, for the first time, the medical experts told me that they believed that this mental health issue was genetic, at least in my family.

Grace's difficult behaviour included targeting James, and blaming him. Grace would raise every bad thing he did, in cruel and hurtful ways. Occasionally, I too would bear the brunt of these irrational moods, and I could not reason with her. The conversations are circular, and Grace continued to fuel her own anger. Jamie was a good target, but he also understood her and was patient and didn't retaliate. He just retreated to his own space.

Chapter Twelve

Extreme Parenting and Stolen Joys

I had always loved children, and I carry the previous generation's beliefs that "all is to be sacrificed for your children". I still strongly believe that childhood experiences are so important, and I have continued working in the community to ensure children have a good life.

I began parenting as a positive and rewarding practice, but it wasn't long before my contact with domestic violence robbed me of my brightest hopes and wishes of a happy family life. Nonetheless, I forged forward, attempting to make the best of my situation with the tenacity that young people possess.

I was far from the perfect mother to my children, and they have reminded me on many occasions. I was very young, had a traumatic childhood, and become a mother as a way to escape a home-life where I was unhappy.

Growing up with Chantel was a fairly easy experience, but not so with Jade who was more challenging. It was difficult raising children in the harsh environment of the mining community of Tom Price, where my partner Charlie was working. Still, I wasn't overly concerned about her, but it pained me that others rejected her as a result of her behaviour. Subjected to the judgement of others, as a mother I began to lose my confidence, and felt that I didn't even have an experience of being parented that I could draw from, to help me out.

Jamie was conceived during the year that we spent living in the mining community. Unlike many families there, we were focused on making the most of the good money that could be made, so we bought a house and settled in. I felt isolated though, as I was away from family and lost my Nana Eve that year. I also didn't take to the life of partying and heavy drinking that is so pervasive within the mining culture.

We got our deposit together, and left to buy our first home in Spearwood, just off Phoenix road. They were happy times, with the kids starting school, renovating our home, lots of swimming in the pool, and celebrations for birthdays. Jade's behaviour did escalate, but starting school helped to occupy her. Despite concerns from the school, Chantel was doing very well academically, and had lots of friends.

Increasingly, I grew isolated from many supports, due to the children's behaviour. Other parents didn't want my children around, and worried that they would influence their children's behaviours. Even as a foster parent, they asked me not to bring Jamie around, as no childcare workers could manage him. It was hard to get even my own family to help out with caring for them.

After a few years, we moved to a larger home on an acre and a quarter in Munster. We had a market garden that grew strawberries, and the property was ideal for us, with large sheds for the trucks, and a very large home with a pool. During this period, we fostered a young boy. We still had some issues, such as Jade's night terrors and Jamie's constant activity and getting into mischief, but overall, we had some fun as a family. I loved the old federation style home, with its wood stove, but equally it had all the modern conveniences. I was very busy during this time, studying, caring for the kids and supporting Charlie in the transport business.

It was during this time that I reconnected with someone I went to school with, Lacey, as we both now faced having all our children at school. Lacey was fun and adventurous, a good counter to my serious, responsible nature, and we often took the children on road trips, planned birthday parties, and, while Charlie was working long hours, she became part of our family. My other friends were concerned about our relationship. They expressed that they felt Lacey was taking over my life, wanting to be me, and have what I had. I didn't listen to the warnings, and didn't realise the impact this would have on my family. Lacey was travelling back and forwards between Western Australia and the eastern states, as her marriage was disintegrating, and she struggled to leave her abusive husband.

It was while here that I began to feel the strain of parenting, as the children approached adolescence. As much as I loved Lacey's company, I began to feel an intrusion on my life, my marriage and my family, as she left her partner. I didn't know how to put good boundaries up and, despite her drinking and impulsive behaviour, I didn't take heed of my uncomfortable feelings. Charlie was still working long hours in our own business, so perhaps Lacey filled my loneliness. I became dependant on Lacey's help, her "can do" attitude, and how she breezed through life without the fears and anxieties that I held, especially around my vulnerability to mental illness.

As much as we loved this home, Charlie and I decided that we wanted to build our own home. The house was sold, and we rented my sister's ex-partner's home, just around the corner. Set on a large block, it was a character, fibro home, surrounded by larger properties, some still operating as market gardens, reminiscent of the ones my grandmother had worked in.

We were a busy household, and flexible, as we almost co-parented the children. Lacey, in leaving her husband, had to leave the two oldest boys with him, and returned to WA with her two youngest boys. Jamie and John had the most remarkable relationship and, like their parents, were opposites in personality. John was playful, fun and well behaved with a great sense of humour, while Jamie delighted in his company. John's death was to have a profound and negative effect on our already vulnerable family.

As the children's behaviour escalated, I parented my children and loved them unconditionally, making it harder to accept that what was happening was not the normal experience of parenting. I watched other parents enjoying being with their children, relaxed and happy. Largely we went on with family life, we took holidays together, celebrated together, and got through the everyday activities.

But I also had to learn to respond to my children in a way that didn't escalate situations. I tempered my emotions, recognising that the more I became upset and distressed, the more the children were not able to calm themselves. It was a skill that was difficult to manage and often judged by others as being passive, allowing my children to behave badly. I never let things ride, though, and always waited till calm was restored. Then I would try to reason with them and gain co-operation. Like all new skills, I failed miserably on many occasions, but was able to achieve my aims, sometimes, by reminding myself it wasn't personal but rather a symptom of my children's inability to manage emotions. This period was also a big learning about how Mum operated, and reminded me of all the times she had been distressed and unable to soothe herself.

I thought deeply about my own parenting, and how I could have a positive impact on my children. A few values, I decided, would help me out in caring for my family. My chosen values were non-violence, honesty, and courage. I don't know the exact process it was that led me to these three, but I knew in my heart that I also had to be a strong role model for them, so I needed to live my values, as much as I could. I instinctively knew that my children would be prone to addiction, so I decided that I could influence them if they saw that I didn't need to use substances to cope.

My children's view of my strategy was not positive. I am sure they saw me as someone who was uptight, critical and judgmental – someone who was averse to anything that was fun and risky. To some degree, that was true. The biggest learning was that, when children enter adolescence, they will drag out all of your own fears, anxiety and unresolved issues, and slap you in the face with them, or wrap you up in them as a distraction from their own behaviour.

My experience of being parented by a mother with Borderline Personality Disorder severely impacted my own development, and I think about my attachment to her in the early years. Possibly, out of all of my siblings, I received the best of my mother's love, as she was initially well, and became more unwell as each child came along. I wonder if that was the protective factor for me, or if, in fact, I saw that her behaviour was not right so never felt a strong connection to her. To this day, I have a difficult relationship with my mum, and experience much guilt about this, but I know that it is my survival mechanism. I love her and forgive her for all that has happened, and feel compassion for her experiences, knowing that she has endured much pain in her life.

I was often required to attend school and supervise Jamie, or to meet with school staff concerning Jade. I had a horrible experience at Chantel's high school with the school nurse who accused me of treating Chantel like the family slave, and not including her. I was shocked, hurt and thankful to the guidance officer who could see that I was a loving mum deeply concerned about a daughter who was engaging in risky behaviours.

Having a normal, settled life was difficult, even with a two-parent family, and life became even more difficult as a single parent. I was not able to work, at times, and even study was not fluid and was often interrupted by the need to support Jamie at school. I was often at the school, on standby to assist if staff needed support to manage him, or if he was not coping and I needed to take him home. Many times, I was powerless to know where he was, or what he was doing, and I could do nothing else but manage my own anxieties.

Despite all of this, I tried to own parts my life, perhaps as with my mother I found it a positive to have something outside of my parenting. I studied, enjoyed it, and worked, at times. This helped me to not become fixated on the problems we had in the family. I was also lucky that I was successful, and this achievement strengthened my sense of self. Having strong future goals also supported me in surviving what was, at times, intense, stressful, and exhausting. I refused to lose myself to Borderline Personality Disorder, although I am able to reflect on how much joy was stolen from my life.

The worst of all my experiences was the emotional exhaustion. I had to deal with situations that were the stuff of nightmares – caring for a child who was constantly suicidal, all of my children engaging in risky behaviours, and not the normal drug use of adolescents. Sometimes I couldn't cope, and I asked Jamie to leave. This, I regret, as it triggered his feelings of abandonment and reinforced his feelings of being worthless. I also left Western Australia without my daughter Chantel, as she refused to come with us. I maintained my relationship with her, but I sometimes reflect how different things might have been if we stayed there.

The exhaustion was pervasive, at times, and was the biggest challenge in maintaining my own emotional health. It struck me most when Jamie had flare-ups and was unwell. I had to put aside my own feelings. This was not as prevalent as when I had to stand aside and watch as systems such as education, health, police and court systems dealt with our family in ways that were not helpful to recovery or supportive of a traumatised child or adult. *What is the "normal' way to react to such extreme circumstances?*

Part Three
For the Love of Jamie

Chapter Thirteen

Something's Happened to the Boy

It was a beautiful, crisp autumn morning. Blue skies beckoned with not a cloud in sight, but the freshness of winter's warning embraced us. My kids dressed and readied themselves for school. They sat waiting for their lift to arrive, as my car had broken down. The crackling of tyres hit the crushed limestone driveway and the scraping and slamming of the van door signalled that Lacey and her kids had arrived. I met her at the front door and asked where her kids had gone.

"They're walking to the shops," Lacey replied. "It's payday, so I'm letting them buy some snacks for school." We entered the lounge room together, chatting away as we waited for her children to get back, so they could all go to school together.

It seemed like only a few minutes passed before we heard a panicked voice calling out at the front door. A man, vaguely familiar but I couldn't place him, stood in the doorway. Struggling to place where I knew him from, I was struck by the look on his face.

He stuttered. "You better come. Something's happened."

I stared blankly, not understanding.

The man grew nervous, shaking. He repeated, "You need to come. Something's happened to the boy."

Lacey joins me in the doorway as my mind fights against the horror I feel inside.

"Which boy?" I ask.

He can't answer, so I ask more gently. "Is it the blonde boy or the dark-haired boy?"

Inside, I'm praying it's not Jamie.

"The dark one," he replies.

My sense of relief only lasts a few seconds as the feeling of total dread takes over. We both follow as he turns and runs back to the shop that he owns. We reach a few metres outside the gate, and I see a scene ahead that looks surreal. Cars, police, and bystanders surround a tiny, curled-up body on the road. We run as Lacey heads to her son on the road, and me to her older son standing on the roadside, frozen in fear.

I feel powerless as I try to help him, a traumatised young boy, back to the house and away from the scene of horror. He is so terrified he is unable to make the step off the kerb onto the road no matter how much I coach him and gently whisper, "It's okay. You can make it."

He wants his Mum. He needs his Mum. Lacey is gently caressing her baby boy, John, as it sets in that he is already gone. She keeps looking over, pleadingly. Her face asks me to take care of it, but I can't. Lacey has to tear herself away from her dead boy, and help get her other child away. She gets him moving, and we steer him back to the house. My guilt at not being able to help keeps telling me I have let my dear friend down.

So much was happening as the police arrived at our house. We tried to organise someone to help out with the other children. Lacey had to call to the boys' dad and arrangements were made to identify the body. It vaguely crossed my mind that Jamie wasn't around, but my usual mother's instinct failed to identify where he was. Eventually, friends from the Salvation Army arrived and helped out. Jamie (who was five at the time) appeared, and he was okay. We began working through the mountain of things that needed to be done. All of this was made more difficult for me by my desire to disassociate from what was happening, and from knowing that my friend needed my support and that I couldn't fail her now.

The following weeks are a blur, and I am sure we all worked through what needed to be done as if in a state of sleep walking. In all honesty I don't remember much, but have a sense of an all-encompassing sadness falling over our household. Rather than a family, it felt like we were strangers occupying the same space but not connecting. This is something that I wish I could go back and change.

A few months later, my cheeky, mischievous boy became an angry, aggressive child, with periods of sadness that I couldn't break through. Things reached boiling point when he threw a brick at his sister, Jade. As he learned how to write, he began writing "I want to die" on bits of paper in his room, on his toybox, and in his reading books. Things at school, of course, were not any better, so I reached out to the children's hospital and made an appointment with a child psychiatrist.

Our first appointment came up quickly. Jamie's father and I sat in the small consulting room talking with the doctor about how we were struggling to manage Jamie's changes in behaviour, and that we thought he needed grief counselling. We left the room while he talked to Jamie alone. After a short while, the doctor called us back in. He told us not to be concerned about the grief, as he felt that Jamie was managing that, but he was very concerned about Jamie's behaviour, which he felt indicated that Jaime may be on the autistic spectrum. I asked the doctor to explain further. He said that Jamie struggled to follow directions and failed to understand social conventions. He gave the example of Jamie walking around the doctor's desk to touch his books in the bookcase behind him. He agreed that there were issues that warranted investigating, and he wanted to do some IQ testing. We attended a few more appointments. They concluded that Jamie had an above average IQ, so they weren't really concerned, but felt he may be a bit hyperactive (I thought this was an understatement). My daughter Chantel also asked to speak to a doctor about her grief, and perhaps this was what triggered our referral to a family therapist.

I believe that family therapy is a wonderful and necessary mode of intervention, but our experience was less than optimal. The first session was awful. My kids were aged six, ten, and twelve, and were not overly co-operative. They spent the whole session throwing toys at each other and laughing, and did not engage in any therapeutic work. The poor therapist took the opportunity to end the session when his pager started beeping, stating he had an emergency and needed to leave. We were never offered another appointment.

The children's hospital didn't seem to have any answers, so, after a break, I arranged a referral to the Child Development Clinic. Coincidentally, the same psychiatrist who'd seen Jade a few years ago, now worked at this clinic.

We attended a few sessions where the therapist mostly made observations. At the fourth session, however, James was really showing the worst of his behaviour. He ran up and down the hallways, slammed doors, and threw toys around. Despite the doctor instructing him to stand still, James continued to run. Finally, the doctor called him back into the room sternly. As Jamie entered, the doctor grabbed him roughly, clasping his upper arms and forcing them close to his body. Jamie stiffened as the doctor picked him up, lifting him a foot off the floor, and shoved him roughly into an armchair.

The doctor turned and looked at me and stated, "That is all you need to do."

I was stunned. I questioned the doctor's actions, stating that he only had Jamie for five minutes in his office that day, while I lived with this day in and day out. If I was to start doing that, I argued, Jamie would end up being abused.

The psychologist replied with all the authority of someone who is not used to being questioned. "Well, if you can't do it, he needs to be in foster care."

I left his office horrified, but I dared not question him further. I also felt that I couldn't withdraw from the intervention, as I knew that Jamie needed it so much.

Jamie remembered this for years afterwards. He would often say, "You're just going to give me away anyway." When we later moved to Queensland, this incident stayed in his mind – that if he kept being naughty, he would be given away. There was very little that was supportive, and even less that was effective, in helping him with this.

This therapist continued to work with us, recommending medication, so, after a long discussion about the pros and cons, Jamie was started on Dexamethamine. I was reluctant, but thought it was worth a try. If it was successful, he could at least engage in school. The trial was very unsuccessful. Jamie reacted badly to the medication. He turned into a zombie, unable to interact at all, and with an extremely low mood.

From age 7 to 11 Jamie was supported to stay in class through Social and Psychological Education Resources (SPER), a team of experienced educators led by a psychologist. Their aim was to work in class, to establish programs that the school could then self-manage. It was hard work, but those amazing people cared for my son and were wonderful advocates. Advocacy became increasingly important, as the Western Australian government decided that if a child had more than 30 days' suspension, they would be excluded from all government schools. In Year Three, Jamie had 18 days suspension days by Easter, and the school made it clear that they would continue to suspend him until he had to be excluded from all schools. We all panicked, and SPER staff attempted to negotiate punitive measures with the school. The school's response was that if SPER did not back off, they would be banned from working with any children in the school.

At home, I was exhausted. My only saving grace was that Jamie was a good sleeper. He was usually up early, though, and one particular day he had got himself dressed and left home at 6:30, while I was in the shower. I got out to find him missing, got dressed and headed out in the car to find him. Driving around the streets of our local suburb, I eventually found him near the school. With much coaxing, I got him in the car. We arrived home only to have him take off again as soon as the car had stopped. Again, I reversed out of the driveway to find him. When I got him home, I settled him in front of the TV while I got the girls organised. It was close to school start time. I don't know what triggered him after he had been so keen to go to school but, suddenly, on the drive to school, he began screaming and kicking, and threatening to jump out of the car. I made it safely to the school carpark, but then he refused to get out. He kicked the dashboard so hard that it cracked. I was afraid to touch him for fear of making him worse, so we sat in the car, me on the verge of tears of frustration while other parents stared on incredulously at us. The feeling of embarrassment didn't even kick in this time, as it had many times before. We were shunned, talked about, and avoided, despite my engagement in school life as a volunteer.

That day, I was at the end of my ability to cope. I started the car up and drove off with tears running down my face, and with Jamie calmly and slowly saying that he wasn't sure what was going to happen next.

I drove straight to Fremantle Hospital. Arriving at the hospital triage, the nurse recognised my distress and immediately came over to us. By this time, Jamie was again hyped up and running around, calling out, and generally attracting attention. I calmly told her that I had had a terrible morning and I didn't know what to do anymore. Jamie had just started under a new paediatrician who he was seeing as a private patient, but I knew she had clinics at the hospital. Without seeing a doctor, they sent me around to the children's ward where they spoke to the registrar who agreed that Jamie should be admitted for observation.

I helped get Jamie settled into a ward by himself, and they said I could go. I was relieved to have someone watch him and hopefully assess what was wrong. The doctor suspected some abnormal brain activity, so an EGG was ordered, including a sleep study.

The next morning when I went to visit him, I noticed that staff were all gathered around his door. As I approached, I thought to myself, *What now?* The staff told me that he had sworn at a nurse and ended up locking the door from the inside, so no one could access the room. I asked what had led up to this. Thinking he was lonely, they'd asked if he wanted to move into a shared ward. As always with Jamie, as he hadn't been prepared for the question, this suggestion had triggered a major reaction. I gently coaxed him to open the door. He did this, but then ran back to hide under the bed again, still swearing at the nurse. I sat on the floor for about fifteen minutes before I coaxed him to come out and move to the shared ward. The mothers there sympathised. They had all heard the commotion. The other children were a bit weary of him, but they tried to engage him in play.

He stayed for a week as a social admission to allow observations and to give our family a break. Every day when I visited, I found him with his socks on, sliding down the hallways, not engaging with anyone, not playing, just delighting in his own company. Tests showed no signs of abnormal brain activity, but they started him on Tegretol to help manage him. This helped only marginally, but it was the best we had at the time.

Chapter Fourteen

Kids that Age Don't try to Kill Themselves

Our move to Queensland provided a new start for Jamie. I hoped that a new State, with a different education system, may be a blessing for him. I had begun to feat that we could no longer keep him engaged in school in WA. He started year 5 in Queensland, attending Clontarf State School. The school was initially impressed how academically he was way ahead of his peers especially in maths, but it wasn't long before his behaviour became the most noticeable feature.

We had been estranged from Lacey and her family for a few years, but while we planned to travel, and she had offered us a place to stay. Within a few weeks of arriving, we were just settling in with the kids at school. I started my first placement in social work, and was looking forward to the new experience.

Early one morning, we received a phone call to say that my daughter Chantel had lost her beautiful baby boy, aged three months. We had to return to Western Australia and support her during this period, although I felt powerless to ease her pain. As a grandparent, I was dealing with my own feelings of loss, but I put them aside and supported Chantel for six weeks. The autopsy delayed the funeral, as we wanted him buried whole, and they eventually determined that our precious little boy had died of SIDS.

I visited the morgue with Chantel every few days, as she held her tiny baby's body and tried to accept what had happened. Often, I couldn't stand to be in the room, and would excuse myself after a few minutes, waiting outside until she was ready to part with him. On many occasions, I held back the nausea as the smells entered my nostrils, wafted into my clothes and burned a memory into my brain that is never forgotten. These are the sacrifices you make for the love of your children. I had bought her a box to keep his clothing and memories safe, knowing this was not likely to ease any of the pain.

During this time, I was able to somewhat repair my relationship with Chantel's in-laws, as cultural misunderstandings had caused conflict. I made a point of consulting them about their traditions, and was privileged and humbled to participate in a yarning circle, as part of Aboriginal Sorry Business. I spoke to a group of these women about motherhood. Out of the all the women there, only two hadn't lost a child in the first year of their life, and none could tell me the cause of all the deaths. These Aboriginal women taught me about their traditions, and that they couldn't understand why us "whitefellas" needed to conduct autopsies. There was a sense of acceptance of life, death, and spirit that was very different from my own. The entire experience brought home the vast difference in health outcomes for Indigenous people.

On returning to Queensland, we again attempted to settle. One of the first things that I did was to engage in some counselling, as I struggled to understand why my grandson was taken and how the authorities had not foreseen the danger to him, withdrawing support to my daughter and her partner a few months before his birth. The neglect, domestic violence, and drug use was still occurring.

Unfortunately, both Jade and Jamie's behaviour began to escalate. Jamie struggled to stay in a classroom as noise and activity worried him. His deputy principal, a wonderful, insightful teacher, took him under her wing. She approached me one day asking if I thought Jamie was a gifted child.

I laughed. "I haven't ever thought that, but he definitely is different." I took to her quickly and trusted her to support my son in the kindest and most compassionate way. She never let me down.

I don't understand why, but August is always a really bad time for my family. Perhaps that's because it marks the anniversary of the life-changing car accident that I was involved in as a child – somehow that trauma has transferred to the next generation.

It must have been a weekend, as I don't remember the kids going to school. Jade and Jamie had been playing upstairs with Lacey's children, and I was busy doing the washing. I went upstairs and found that Jamie wasn't there. The kids said they didn't know where he was. I went downstairs and called out to him, but no answer.

He is covered in vomit, lying on my double bed. I run to him. I think to myself he must have a tummy bug, although he was rarely sick, even with the usual childhood illnesses. I help him to the shower. He is groggy but conscious. As I turn the shower on, he loses consciousness. I struggle to hold him up, and yell for help. Charlie arrives. Understanding the urgency, I yell, "We have to get him to hospital! He's passed out!" We wrap him in a towel, and I grab him in my arms while Charlie gets into the driver's seat. On my lap, Jamie begins fitting. I am terrified, screaming, "Go faster!" to Charlie. Luckily, the hospital is less than three kilometres away. We arrive and Jamie is taken into emergency immediately, as he is still unconscious and having seizures.

Staff escort Charlie and me into the little room that I know they use for families when there is bad news. I sit there trembling. Charlie tries to comfort me, but he too is in shock. I don't know what Charlie was thinking, but my mind was saying over and over, *We are going to lose him, we are going to lose him.*

I can see my son's thin, lifeless body on the bed, pale and still. Doctors gather saying they can't find out what is wrong, and they need to do more tests. Then they will transfer him to the children's hospital. They request consent to do a lumber puncture to check his spinal fluid, and we agree without hesitation. The next few hours are painful as we sit with our worst thoughts.

Jamie eventually comes to, slowly, but he is sedate and quiet – so unlike my boy. He is stable now, and can be transferred to the Royal Brisbane Children's Hospital. It is late at night, and the hospital staff suggest we go home, while they wait to transfer him by ambulance. They tell me that he will be okay until morning.

Early the next morning, I travel to Brisbane to see my boy. Jamie is still very quiet, for him, but some of his old, cheeky spark is back. I talk to the doctors and they tell me that he had taken an overdose of his medication Tegratol. That has caused his seizures. I am shocked and horrified. Jamie is eleven years old. *Kids that age don't try to kill themselves, do they?*

Doctors confirm that blood tests indicate Jamie has taken around twenty or more tablets. I am numb, not knowing what to say or ask. This was the beginning of having to always determine safety at home, locking up medications, knives and any other implements that may be used in suicide attempts, monitoring his moods and trying to keep him safe.

A few hours later, they say he can go home. I pack Jamie up and we leave – no questions, no advice from staff or doctors, and no referrals for any follow up. But, then again, I am still numb. Perhaps the staff felt I was not up to further information at that stage.

I found out later from the kids at home that Jamie was being bullied by his sister Jade, and by Lacey's son. Their behaviour was the trigger to Jamie's first suicide attempt. Quickly after that, we moved from Lacey's home.

Ongoing problems at school drove me to seek more support for Jamie. I contacted Child and Youth Mental Health Services (CYMHS). His intake meeting was telling. He talked about his behaviour not mattering because, if he was naughty, he would be given away. I saw his thinking as the lasting impact on a young child's mind from less than satisfactory intervention. Thankfully, we had some very committed workers during this time, workers who encouraged me to feel confident and who tried to ensure that Jamie understood that "he was okay". Intervention at that stage largely depended on the skills of the individual workers, but the staff roster was frequently rotated.

The following year, almost to the day, another incident impacted our family, especially Jamie. We were living in a house near bushland. Jamie was always exploring and often went missing for hours as we couldn't contain him. He remained constantly anxious, fidgety, and on the move. By this stage, the developmental clinic at the children's hospital was also involved in Jamie's treatment. Staff there diagnosed him with PTSD and Asperger's Syndrome. Although the specialist stated that something didn't quite fit with ASD, he explained that the diagnosis would enable additional supports for Jamie at school. He was placed on Zoloft, an anti-depressant. We will never know if taking antidepressants contributed to his downward spiral and the events that followed, but there is a risk of suicidal thoughts in young people who take this medication.

That day, Jamie arrived home not too late, so we were not concerned. He was twelve, but very independent. He burst through the door quickly and headed straight into the bathroom, without making eye contact or talking. I heard the shower start and, next thing, there was an almighty scream, like he was being murdered.

I race into the bathroom and look at him. He is standing there, dripping wet and naked, with huge blisters forming on his face, shoulders and chest. He is burnt. Charlie and I comfort him and, again, race him to the hospital. He tells us that he was playing with petrol and set fire to himself. We can't get out of him if it was an accident or on purpose. Jamie was alone when he hurt himself, so nobody was around to help. He ran home, thinking he would get in trouble, so he didn't tell us, just got in the shower. He kept it together until the pain of the water striking the burns overwhelmed him.

Again, at emergency, Jamie is treated immediately and admitted to the children's ward at our local hospital. I stay to get him settled into the ward, and head home after a long day. I promise him I will see him in the morning before I start work.

Before 8am, I am back at the hospital. A male nurse appears to be in charge of the ward alone. He does not look too happy. I watch as Jamie pushes wheelchairs over to the doors in an attempt to escape. I thwart his attempts and try to distract him and make him laugh. It doesn't work. After putting down the phone, the nurse approaches me.

"We don't have facilities for kids like him," the nurse says.

I feel insulted. "What do you mean?"

"We can't look after kids like him here." The look on the nurse's face screams *don't mess with me*.

I collect Jamie's belongings and return home, ringing work to say that I can't come in.

For a child who was sensitive to touch, severe burns were horrific. He screamed and screamed, and I feared that he would get an infection as I couldn't get him to sit still or allow me to treat his injuries properly. For three Days, I tried to manage his wounds. Things got worse. Psychologically, he was deteriorating. He paced around the room, calling himself hateful names, and saying he wanted to die.

Through tears and sobs, he finally told me that he saw his friend die. He saw John hit by the car and told me that it was his own fault. There was nothing I could do that would convince him otherwise.

I knew I could no longer care for him. I drove into the city to the children's hospital and we were seen almost immediately. The doctor said they would keep him in the burns unit for a few days, until they had an available bed at the Child and Family Therapy Unit (CAFTU).

On admission, the staff explained how Jamie's burns had re-triggered trauma experienced when his friend had died. They told me and that Jamie's distress was high. Jamie's developmental specialist, Dr Briggs, decided to increase his anti-depressants – he doubled the dose. Days later, Jamie's distress increased, until he required 24-hour nursing. Staff feared he would harm himself. I fought back tears of helplessness as I watched him stand on the timber ledge and bash his head against the glass, screaming, "I want to die! Just let me die!"

After a week, Jamie's burns began to heal. He was transferred to CAFTU. I visited daily and saw many psychiatrists, psychologists, and nurses. Together with Dr Briggs, they attempted to assess Jamie's condition. I recall one time overhearing Dr Briggs and other professionals screaming at each other in the hallway, as they argued about Jamie's treatment.

During his stay, despite it being a locked ward, Jamie could not be contained. Staff regularly called to tell me that he was missing, and that security was looking for him. Jamie spent his time surveying the hospital grounds, a curious behaviour that he repeated wherever we went. A few hours later, they called again to say he had been returned. Years later, Jamie told me that every time they found him, they placed him in restraints.

As it came time to discharge Jamie, the consultant psychiatrist met with me. He was very kind, as he spoke to me about the future. He said that, as a parent, I was doing all that could be done and, like many professionals before him, he admitted to me that they didn't have any answers for me. He said that it may be possible to trial Lithium to stabilise him. I asked what they knew about using this drug, commonly used for bi-polar disorder, in children.

The psychiatrist replied, "We know nothing."

I left disheartened, but decided not to allow my son to be a guinea pig, as they didn't know the about the effects on people so young.

Finally, the psychiatrist said, "Things will get worse. It is very likely that Jamie will suicide in his teen years."

I felt the colour drain from my face but, in my heart, I knew that this was a moment of brutal truth that I could not turn away from. So started my determination to do everything in my power to prevent my young son from taking his life. I knew, though, that I didn't have control, and that if he decided to follow through and was determined to end it, I could not stop him.

Chapter Fifteen

Brother

By this stage, Jamie had already started smoking and engaging in drug use. He was desperate for smokes and would do almost anything to get them, including stealing. Pot was also available through his friends and, for those parents who think, *not my child*, I want to assure you that you can't know for certain. Most of Jamie's friends had older brothers who were using marijuana regularly, and the younger ones would sneak some and share it. This was common among Jamie's friends, even at age eleven and still in primary school.

It was during this time that Charlie and I separated. Jamie came to live with me in a little unit I rented. While upset with the separation, Jamie recognised that I was not happy, and he let me know that it was okay, as long as he could still see his dad. I agreed that this was the most important thing, and Charlie and I both remained supportive of each other and Jamie.

CYMHS was a constant support for the next few years, although many workers came and went. Some workers said that Jamie's smoking was okay and that, in some ways, it helped to calm the brain. Supporting this theory was the high number of people with mental health issues who smoked so much. Well, times change, and before long I became targeted as a "bad parent" for allowing him to smoke. I didn't supply the cigarettes, in fact, I gave up smoking myself to discourage him.

The units where we lived where on the waterfront at Hornibrook Esplanade, Clontarf. Jamie loved being near the water and fishing. In fact, myself and his deputy principal often drove down to the waterfront looking for him when he absconded from school. He also spent hours alone, fishing at woody point jetty, a pastime that he loved and inherited from his dad.

Our neighbours were friendly. An older Fijian Indian lady lived upstairs. Her brother sometimes visited, riding his pushbike into the driveway and leaving it against the brick wall near our door, while he saw his sister. The man seemed friendly, and I wasn't immediately concerned, until a male friend visitor told me he knew this person. My friend disclosed that the man had been involved in the local football club and that he was a team manager. Heavily involved in the team himself, my friend warned me that it was known that this man had taken kids from his team to Dreamworld and sexually abused at least one boy. My friend had tried to raise this with the club, but was shunned. He'd also received a letter from the man's lawyer, threatening to take legal action for defamation. My friend had then shut his mouth until the day he warned me not to let Jamie anywhere near him. I agreed, and I also decided not to speak out as I didn't want to be threatened with legal action either. I spoke to Jamie and warned him to never be alone with that man. I explained that sometimes some people were not safe to be with. I made Jamie promise me, which he did.

One day, Jamie came home all excited, saying that this man was going to buy him a new bike. I was astounded and felt uneasy, not only because Jamie had spoken to him, but because this man was being so seemingly generous. I felt suspicious, as I recalled my friend's words. I called Charlie, and told him the story and my concerns. I told him that I didn't want Jamie left alone with this man at all. We decided that Charlie would go with Jamie to see the man and to check the situation out. They both met him at the bike shop where Jamie picked out the bike he wanted. Jamie was so excited when he got home, yet I felt so deflated. I had hoped that Charlie may have sensed that this situation was not right and spoken sternly to the man. But Charlie was taken by the man's work that he did for the community, and he didn't sense anything untoward.

Brother

It wasn't too long after that Jamie and I moved to a new home. Jade had decided to stay with her Dad, as she couldn't stand Jamie at that stage. She was still defiant and had begun drinking. She didn't take to Charlie's new girlfriend much and, at one stage, threatened her, upsetting her dad. We remained in close contact, but she swore she would never live with Jamie again.

It was my first mortgage on my own. Jamie and I soon settled into our old, but well-loved, workers' cottage. Jamie had made friends at school, and he often spent weekends hanging out with them. I knew that they occasionally smoked pot and, despite my stance on an alcohol- and drug-free house, I couldn't monitor him all the time. Jamie became distant and stopped talking to me at home. In other ways, he remained the same little man who wrapped himself up in his quilt and would not allow me to wash his clothes. He wore the same jocks, day in and day out. They felt comfortable, but could almost have walked themselves into the washing machine.

One day, Jamie was obviously stoned when he returned home. As I had many times before, I told him that I was worried about him. He blurted out how the man who'd given him the bike had taken him and his friend to a hotel room where he had tried to film them, but the video camera was broken. I tried to remain calm, instinctively knowing that, if I freaked out, he would close down. I didn't get much more out of him about that incident, but I knew this wasn't good.

I contacted the police immediately and provided them with the name of the person and Jamie's friend who had been with him. The police raided the man's home. They agreed with me that he was a paedophile, as they found video of him having sex with a 17-year-old. The offender claimed, however, that the boy had told him he was eighteen, so no charges were laid. Detectives also questioned Jamie's friend who they said gave a very good account of the sexual abuse that had occurred. Unfortunately, this boy's mother was uncooperative and the police knew, as I did, that Jamie would not make a good witness due to his developmental and mental health issues. The stress and trauma of a court battle would negatively impact on Jamie's emotional wellbeing and the officers advised me that, even with two credible child witnesses, they would only have a 50% chance of convicting the man.

Jamie's many incarcerations began at aged fourteen, after he was introduced to amphetamine (speed). Jamie described to me the day that a forty-year-old man had injected him. Without bitterness, he said that he knew it was wrong, but that he wanted to belong, be part of something, be accepted, even if it was with a group of people who others would shun. The feeling of being "normal" that he got from the drugs was a bonus for Jamie. Many times, I saw my son acting with confidence, laughing and joking. I didn't doubt for a minute that he was self-medicating. Years before, at the beginning of his drug use, some mental health staff had advised me to remove all medications from him, due to his illicit drug use.

With the drug use, came increased risk for self-harm and accidents. He increased his criminal activity too, to pay for speed. On a few occasions, Jamie stole cars, but he usually pulled up when the police followed him. I spoke to a psychologist about this, and he explained that stealing cars was much like drug use. It pumped the young people full of adrenaline, giving them a buzz.

One incident, which I didn't know about until many years later, happened as a result of Jamie's impulsive and reckless behaviour. Jamie had stolen something from a drug dealer, and he was caught out. As revenge, they toyed with him for hours, holding a gun to his head and threatening to shoot him. As if that wasn't enough, they then placed him in the boot of a car, driving around with him like that for a few days, before they finally thought he had endured enough, and released him. I remember this time well, as he had been missing and we were extremely worried. When he turned up, his dad was so angry, he hit him. I never agreed with any violence and, when I think back, I hate that this happened to Jamie. I understand that his dad did it due to stress, but I was still horrified. After what Jamie had been through, he needed love and support. Instead he was met with more violence. It was no wonder Jamie didn't tell me till years later. My heart beats wildly as I write this, and I hope that those who did this to my son rot for their actions.

I don't defend Jamie's crimes at all. I always taught him to take responsibility for his actions. There were times I wanted to scream at the experiences that both Jamie and we, as a family, had to endure. An early example was when Jamie was taken in for questioning and the detective failed to check his file for any alerts, such as suicide risk. The police left Jamie alone in the interview room, only to come back and find him hanging from the camera in the corner of the room. Jamie had removed the lace from his shorts and hung himself. Luckily, the officers weren't gone for long. They cut him down quickly, albeit with a very strong, red mark around his neck. The detectives contacted us immediately and could not apologise enough when we arrived. They explained, as so many people had said to me before, that Jamie "looked normal", and they didn't realise he had any issues. I guess this is the way with mental health, nobody sees it.

Throughout his teens, Jamie spent time in the old, decommissioned youth detention centre. He was also one of the first group at the new Youth Detention Centre at Wacol, in Brisbane's west. We were regular visitors there, and I still feel sad at the small number of families who visit their children. We became well known, due to our regular visits. We also became known for complaining about processes that were not family friendly. Luckily, our complaints were seen for the offers of feedback that they were, so vital to helping encourage other families to visit.

Visiting detention centres with young children is controversial. Erin was only two years old when I brought her with me to visit Jamie. It wasn't a scary place for her, as she was focused on seeing her "brother". Erin, being somewhat indulged, never used Jamie's name, but rather referred to him in terms of the place he held in the family, relevant to her. "Brother" was her favourite person, and she was always so happy to see him that they had a ritual. Erin would run at him and he would hoist her into his arms. She got so good at this, she was able to launch herself waist height and throw her legs around his hips and her arms around his neck, as he twirled her around. She kept this up until she was about eleven. Only one guard complained about it, asking them to separate. I understand the guard's reaction, as there were men that would not have seen this as innocent love between a sister and brother, and it may have triggered deviant thoughts or actions, but this was just how my children connected.

I attended an open day at the Youth detention Centre. I was the only parent in attendance. The staff were so happy to share the programs that Jamie was completing and his achievements. I came home with a coffee table he had made. The psychologist sought me out and told me how glad he was that I had come. He wanted to talk to me. Pulling me into an office, he told me that Jamie was different to most of the kids in detention. He said that Jamie had "a heart of gold", something I already knew.

The psychologist told me that "Jamie wouldn't be alive if it wasn't for you and his Dad."

"Thank you," I replied, holding back tears and trying to listen, in case he could give me some answers.

He went on the say, "I have no doubt that Jamie would have suicided, but he loves you so much he can't do it. It would hurt you too much, and he doesn't want that."

I sat stunned and wordless. How do you answer something so profound?

"I love him so much, too," I said.

He went on, gently, talking about not making Jamie feel too guilty about what happens, and to always make Jamie's safety a priority. This is something I had already decided. It didn't matter if he didn't finish school, it didn't matter if he was in detention, it *mattered* that he was alive and that, if we could keep him alive, there would always be hope.

Another beautiful soul working at the detention centre was an elderly man. I remember him saying he was in his seventies, though I can't remember his name. The old man was a community visitor, and he encouraged the relationship between Jamie and Erin, in such a meaningful and beautiful way. He got Jamie to read fairy tales and record them, so they could be sent to Erin to listen to. This amazing man, I believe, nurtured the most beautiful relationship, in such a simple way. I remember speaking to him about why he did this work. He asked me to think back to when I was in school, and tell him the name of a child that was always in trouble. It was an easy thing to do. He said he also remembered these and wondered how horrible it must be for those, usually boys, who were seen, daily, as "the naughty boys".

Like the rest of life, there were periods when Jamie was not in detention, and periods where he was more stable, mentally, and our family life was settled. During these times, Jamie was like every other boy, involved in education, training, and chasing girls. At fourteen, though, he was at his worst. He had grown rapidly to nearly six foot, had experienced trauma that would be unfathomable, and he was using drugs heavily. At one stage we begged the magistrate to give him a custodial sentence, as we feared he would die. He weighed about 40 kilos, and didn't care if he lived or died. He also contracted Hepatitis C and the bacterial "superbug", MSRA.

Staff at CYMHS swayed between a number of diagnoses, including PTSD, Conduct Disorder, and Oppositional Defiance Disorder (ODD), but nothing was ever concluded and opinions changed depending on the latest research, policy, or worker's knowledge and areas of interest. The one thing that I didn't like, due to our previous experience, was dealing with psychiatrists. I would clearly state this and refused them, if it was just a routine visit. Only if they gave a valid argument for psychiatric assessment would I consent. As a parent, I believe it is your right to choose the types of intervention and indeed if any intervention is required for your child. A strategy I developed was to take breaks from intervention when they weren't working, or if Jamie had become tired. I believe it is important for families to develop their own understanding and resilience, and to maintain some sense of control.

This in-between age is very difficult and, while Jamie didn't actively attempt to harm himself, I know that he didn't care if he did. We tried to give him more love and let him know that we cared, although we couldn't even begin to understand his experiences. Amid the trauma, lovely family memories remain of my beautiful boy and my children's loving brother. Grace adored her big brother, and wanted to follow him everywhere. Jamie enjoyed playing with words. He would play games, like replace words with "Meredith". With Grace, instead of saying her name, he rhymed it, calling her "Gracey, pacey, macey…" This always made Grace laugh. Years later, he continued their sweet relationship, writing beautiful letters to Grace from prison. He'd tell her how wonderful she was, how proud of her he was and how she could be anything she wanted to be. Grace used these letters as motivation. In her last year at school, when didn't want to go, she knew her brother wanted a better opportunity and life for his little sister than he'd had.

Jamie started to see a few girls. He was always popular, and, for a short while these relationships stabilised him. Often, though, the girls he got into relationships with were also traumatised, and their bonds became destructive. If ever there was an issue that placed distance within Jamie and my relationship, domestic violence was it. Jamie became a controlling boyfriend. I was quick to pull him up, but he rebelled, stating that I "always chose the girl's side". I couldn't get him to see that women felt fearful when he behaved in such a bullying way. There was an incident where his girlfriend bit him and he bit her back. She had him charged. I remember talking to her support worker. The worker indicated that girls were often the aggressors. I said, "I don't care. My son knows what is right and what is wrong." The worker was surprised that I had such strong views and also that I had taught my son this.

A very public suicide attempt came when, at one stage, she tried to end the relationship. Jamie threw himself out on the road, in front of a car. He was hit and broke his elbow, requiring an operation where pins were inserted to put it back in place. He tried to throw himself into traffic on a number of occasions. I believe this was part of him playing out his original trauma. Jamie's actions were often impulsive and, as he later told me, "I don't really want to die. I want the pain to stop."

Chapter Sixteen

... Just Another Junkie

I struggled with the legal system and experienced things that I know I will never get over completely. I have always believed and continue to believe in a strong legal system, but I'm also painfully aware how systems can get things wrong, and how this often leads to further abuse of those caught up in them. I have tremendous respect for officers who uphold the law, and through my experiences I've met many who cared very much for the community they served. Unfortunately, I have also experienced those who are at the very least over-stressed, reactive and overwhelmed with their work, or who have been reduced to a person who sees policing as a way to exert power over others. As he grew into an adult, the way that James was treated changed. The mixture of mental illness and drug use is not understood by most officers, and this lack of understanding increases stressors on offenders and the probability of violence towards both police and offenders alike.

My first experience of this led me to become very worried when Jamie was in custody. Not only was this the time for highest suicide risk, as the shame and guilt would hit Jamie, but it was also the time of most risk of police violence. Just after Jamie turned eighteen, he was taken into custody at Redcliffe Police Station. I received a call, if I recall correctly quite late in the evening, stating that they had Jamie in custody. I asked how he was doing, and they said he was in good spirits, so I thanked them and said I would be down in the morning to see him before court. I went to bed relieved that Jamie was good and safe for now.

On the Border

At 8 in the morning I arrived at the lock-up and was allowed to see Jamie. I was shocked at his physical state. He had a large white swelling on his forehead, about 5cm by 4cm. He had swelling to both his knees, although the bruising hadn't begun to appear, and other sites on his body indicated that he had been hit. Most shockingly, he had red marks and bruising and swelling around his neck, behind his ears, going up into his hairline. These marks, I know, are usually caused by strangulation, as I had learnt in relation to Domestic Violence training. As I was behind the glass, I couldn't even hug him or do anything to relieve his pain or fear in his eyes. We placed our hands together against the glass, and I held back my tears, asking him what happened.

"It doesn't matter, Mum," Jamie said.

"It's so wrong. Who did this?" I asked him.

Jamie looked into my eyes and said, "Mum, let it go. It just makes it worse if you complain."

I had to end the visit as I knew I could no longer contain the anger I felt. I asked to be released, and the officer quickly opened the door. I looked back to see Jamie hanging his head, unable to look at me.

Outside, when the door shut, I turned to the officer and said sternly, "What happened in there?"

The officer was an older man I had seen before. He looked at me with kindness and, looking down, said, "You know I can't tell you anything. You need to see the Station Officer."

I knew that he had heard what had occurred, but was not able to share with me. I was thankful for his compassion.

I immediately presented at the Police Station desk and asked to see the superintendent about an incident in the lock-up. The officer said he would get him. He came back saying that he wasn't in the office, so I demanded that I speak to the next person in charge. The officer replied that that was him. I explained what I had observed and my previous conversations with a female officer the night before. He stated that he didn't know what had occurred, and would look into it. I stood my ground and said, "I will wait." He left for approximately ten minutes, coming back to tell me that Jamie had caused his injuries himself. I was shocked, but undeterred. I argued that it was possible that Jamie did self-harm, as that was his history, and that it might explain the injuries to his head, knees and other parts of his body, but I was clear, "It is not possible for him to cause strangulation injuries, such as bruising and swelling to the back of his ears and neck." The officer looked weary and defeated. He explained that he would get further information. He left again and came back, enlivened.

"He resisted arrest," the officer said.

I replied that I found this highly unusual, as Jamie had always been compliant with police and this was not consistent with his behaviour.

"So, did you charge him with resisting police?" I asked.

"No," replied the officer.

"I want to make an official complaint," I said.

The officer becomes more official, now stating to me that, as Jamie is over eighteen, he has to make the complaint himself.

I glared at him. "...And you know he won't do that, because he is scared!" Furious, I turn and leave, knowing that I can't hold on to this anger, anger that even if he had caused his own injuries, which I seriously doubted, that no medical treatment was sought. I later heard rumours that the female officer that had called me had been responsible for the injuries, but they couldn't tell me if that was before she called me or after.

There were many arrests and incarcerations during which no issues occurred, and Jamie was mostly dealt with fairly and safely. I was nearly always advised when he was taken into custody, and, as this was usually locally, they knew I was a concerned mother who would visit him as soon as possible. I nearly always attended court as a support for him. Jamie was often placed on "suicide watch" in detention, and also as an adult in the lock-up and prison systems and, although Jamie hated it, as he got older he became less of a suicide risk, but this was sometimes dependant on his circumstances at the time.

One of the big challenges was getting mental health support for Jamie as an adult. As a child and adolescent, he had years of intervention, since the age of five, but suddenly, as an adult, they said that he had to fix his drug issues and then they would help him. I find this ridiculous, as he had mental health issues prior to drug issues. The other problem was that there was limited understanding about dual diagnosis, and even less in terms of treatment programs. Most of his mental health assessments were done by prosecution department staff who stated that he had "Anti-social Personality Disorder, but, as with most people suffering trauma, Jamie never talked of his experiences in life, and time was not taken to speak to family to make these informed assessments. I remember once asking his solicitor for a copy of one of these reports. He looked at me, saying, "There is nothing relevant in there to Jamie or to your family, Amanda. It's best you don't look at it." I was thankful for his empathy and understanding. Not always are these reports reflective of a person's lived experience, although the courts place much value in them.

I spent many hours at hospitals with Jamie when he was in crisis and suicidal, hours of waiting in large, busy, emergency departments with a young person suffering psychosis or suicidal thoughts. The hours of waiting would usually result in Jamie wanting to leave, not able to wait or contain himself. These were the dangerous times, when he would usually be frustrated, leave my care, and engage in risky behaviours. His drug use by now had become more extreme, and I always said to him that "Now you don't actively try to suicide, but you use drugs in such a way that, if it happens, you don't really care."

The second major incident with Jamie happened again in Redcliffe. It had been a bad day, and I was worried about Jamie, as I hasn't seen him much. I got a call from a stranger who stated that he had Jamie's wallet and phone, and he knew that Jamie had been assaulted over a drug debt, but didn't know where he was. The male, I think a friend of Jamie's, said he would keep the wallet, and he gave his phone number if we wanted to pick it up. I did not panic, as I had somewhat become accustomed to assessing what was an immediate concern and when to worry that I might need to take action for Jamie's safety. It was only a few hours later when I got a call from the police, saying that they had Jamie in custody. I asked how he was, and told them that I knew he had been assaulted earlier. They said he was okay. It was about 7pm, and I asked them if they would be charging him. They replied, "Depends on how he behaves," I was puzzled at this, but I rarely questioned their actions after the last experience. I asked that, if they released him, could they call me, so I could bring him home. They agreed to let me know. I told them that, if I didn't hear, I would be down at 8am to see him. I went to bed, thinking he was safe for now, and that they would call if he was let out. Waking up, I had breakfast and headed down to the lock-up. I arrived and my usual knock on the door alerted the officer who came out and told me that Jamie wasn't there. I was stunned. I didn't understand what was happening. The officer looked at me, mumbled something about the prison bus, broke eye contact, and went inside. I still didn't understand what was happening, so I followed him into the station.

I met with a friend, a civilian working for the police who asked, "Are you here to see Jamie?"

I nodded, and she continued, "I saw him before walking through to the cells with bandages over his head."

"What?" I asked. "I have been down there, and they said he's not there."

She said she could go down and check, so I agreed. She was only gone a few minutes when she came back, mystified. She said that they told her "It's none of your business" when she asked if he was there.

I asked her to get the superintendent for me, and she left to do that. She returned, saying that she was told that Jamie was in hospital, but would not disclose which hospital, and that he had refused to see me.

My anger towards the police came secondary to my fears for Jamie. I headed up to the local hospital, arriving at the ED, and enquired if Jamie was there. They were friendly and said that he was, but that he was under guard. They advised that he had head injuries, but they were happy for me to see him. The nursing staff went off and came back looking annoyed. They had been advised that police refused to allow me to see him. I was stonewalled, and my anger reached boiling point. I had always told my boy that he had to take responsibility, yet here I was with others who quite blatantly had not considered their duty of care to my son. This was the first time that I felt compelled to find out the whole story and not let this rest. I had previously drafted a letter to the CMC, but Jamie had begged me not to send it, knowing he would be in custody again and fearing reprisals.

When I was finally able to have a phone call with Jamie, he told me that he didn't remember what happened, but that he was found at 4pm in a car with head injuries. He was charged with breaking into the car, and police reports indicated that he had been waving a stick, threatening in public, and he was charged with this also. What actually occurred that night will never be known, but I do know that the police tried very hard to prevent my contact with my son. I understand he was taken, with head injuries, and placed in front of the magistrate, with the aim of getting him out to the prison hospital immediately. Jamie's solicitor and I urged him to seek to have the charges dealt with through the Mental Health Court, but Jamie hated delays, and living with charges with court pending, so he pleaded guilty.

Jade was married in 2010, and this was the only time I had all of my children together, ever. The day was with the usual stressors of a wedding day, but I also had some concern over my eldest daughter, Chantel, who hadn't been around the family for years and was getting into drugs, together with Jamie. Happily, we all had a wonderful time, and I left thinking that Jamie had heeded my warning about drinking, and all were socialising well.

Chantel came home with us, and Jamie went home with his girlfriend. He had a friend staying overnight. In the early hours of morning, I received a call from the friend saying that Jamie had gone nuts and was taken by the police. He said that he had videoed Jamie, as he was shocked by his behaviour. I explained that he must be in psychosis, but that he would now be safe. That wasn't the end. I received another call from Jamie around 4pm saying he was outside the police station in Caboolture. He asked if I could come and get him, as he had been beaten. Tired and frustrated, I said to Jamie, "It's always something." He said that he was struggling to breathe, and needed a doctor, as he thought that he had broken ribs. He was also frozen with fear that the police were standing there, watching him, from the front of the station, and that they would get him again. I dragged myself out of bed, tired and upset. I picked Jamie up, and we went immediately to the hospital where he was treated and x-rayed. No breaks were noted, but he was covered in bruising to every part of his body. I knew this involved more than one person. I took Jamie home and, the next day, found out that police had removed him from the home, as his partner had reported aggressive behaviour. Police took him to station for the four hours, but didn't charge him at that stage.

The next day, I called the police to discuss what had happened. They took me through the events of the night. They stated that he was removed for his partner's safety, and held in the watchhouse for a few hours. They stated that, on his release, he had stood in front of cars on King Street, asking them to hit him. I asked the officer if they had asked for a mental health assessment, and they said they had completed the 100-point check, three times, and that there were no indications that he was mentally unwell. I challenged this by saying that most people don't stand in traffic asking to be killed. He replied, "He was trying to piss us off." I didn't understand his reasoning. I told him that Jamie had a history of trauma, and had lost his friend who was hit by a car. I said that, "If he chooses to die, he is likely to replay this event." The officer replied, "Well, we are not mental health professionals." I said, "Yes, I know, that was why you should have called someone." The officer grew very angry with me at this and replied, "Well, he broke an officer's wrist," and hung up.

I felt like I was going crazy, speaking to them. They didn't feel accountable. And they didn't understand the things that they had to deal with, especially around mental health, although they must face this on a daily basis. I guess I had assumed that police would have a base knowledge in the signs of mental illness, but that is not so.

We had Jamie home for two days. He was irritable and distressed. I tried to keep him calm, but with extra family members, including my Dad and daughter in a small home, things became strained. My Dad had some honest discussions with me about Jamie, and how he had always thought that Jamie was just spoilt. For the first time, he had seen that Jamie was really unwell, and Dad apologised for not being more supportive.

The effects of Jamie's psychosis came to a head when Grace became scared of him, and we went to leave the house, and he wouldn't let us. I knew I had to call an ambulance and get him to hospital. I did this and, after the immediate reaction of anger from Jamie, he knew he needed to be assessed. When the ambulance and four police cars and the dog handler arrived, Jamie was sitting on the porch waiting to go peacefully with them.

The dog handler was an ex-detective who had known Jamie as a juvenile. He approached Jamie in a friendly and personable way, making a connection with him. He talked about not having heard from Jamie for some time, and how he must have been doing well, and how it was a shame that he was unwell now. After everyone left, the ex-detective approached me and said, "You know, nothing happened down there the other night." I replied, "You have your opinion, and I have mine." He continued, "We don't do those things anymore, not since the case at the Whitsundays." I turned to him, looking him straight in the face, and said, "Just the fact that you, a dog handler, is trying to convince me that nothing happens, indicates to me that it did. There has been talk and you are trying to smooth things over." He changed the subject and we engaged in small talk about Jamie and his triggers, before the officer and his dog left.

To this day, I have Jamie's scribblings from within his prison cell when he was placed in protection among high profile prisoners. Jamie was sent there after they were unable to protect him from being bashed. Jamie had been involved in using drugs in prison and, in an attempt not to get caught, he had flushed a needle and syringe down the toilets. Revenge was swift, and he was bashed, and bashed again in the prison hospital, so he was transferred to high protection. This further traumatised Jamie, as his writing indicates, and he also talked to me about how disgusted he felt when he listened to the way the paedophiles talked to each other. It made me sick to the stomach, and I can only imagine what Jamie must have felt during that time.

It was after this that I noticed Jamie's mental health declining. He got into a relationship with a girl who had also been diagnosed with Borderline Personality Disorder. They had a long friendship, since their early teens, and I know that Jamie wanted a stable life, a relationship, and children. Jamie had received his diagnosis as few years before and had, to some degree, understood his behaviour. Like with most Borderlines, being in a relationship unsettles them further so, after a period of being settled, he was again declining. She, too, was engaging in dramatic and very public suicide attempts.

I remember the night that my own mental health took a dramatic turn as the weariness and pain from dealing with long-term caring was having an impact. Not only was I caring for Jamie, but I had a lot of worry about Grace's self-harming, and her future. I remember being in my room. I bent down and I had this thought come into my head, *Just kill yourself; you are no good to anyone.* The intensity of the thought surprised me, and I couldn't understand where it had come from. It wasn't actual words, I was not hearing voices, it was like a thought from deep within me that had risen to the surface. I didn't feel the impulse to act on it, but I knew that I was in trouble mentally. I immediately saw a doctor, and began anti-depressant treatment. My mood lifted straight away.

Chapter Seventeen

Final Days

It was August 2013, and Jamie appeared in court knowing he was facing a custodial sentence. I was at work and I knew that this time was critical for Jamie. I called Melaleuca clinic to let them know he was in custody, so that they could ensure that he received his dose. In Queensland, addicts can receive doses of Methadone and Suboxone, a drug used to treat opioid addiction, while in the watchhouse, but not in prison. So, entry into prison usually means a rapid withdrawal, which leads to physical and mental symptoms, such a vomiting, nausea, dizziness, diarrhoea, muscle aches, weakness, and lethargy.

I called the watchhouse and spoke to Jamie who was in good spirits, relieved that his dose would be provided. As I hung up the phone and returned to my work, I realised that I had forgotten to say happy birthday to him. I rang back and told the Officer who said he had been taken up to the court, but she would tell him when he got back. We had a laugh together about it not being the best way to celebrate his 28th birthday, but that he seemed happy enough.

He was sentenced to three months, and our life settles into a routine. Jamie still rings me daily, but not with the urgency of his previous calls from prison. There were no demands for money, so I presumed that he was not accessing drugs in prison, as he had previously. He was positive and talked about keeping busy, and engaging in workshops. He did describe feeling so sick one weekend that he couldn't get out of bed, but said he was okay. He was looking forward to getting out and seeing us all, and he re-enforced that his family was everything to him. We talked about Grace, as she was finishing year 10 and looking forward to all the end of year activities. I told him how his letters inspired her to do well. Jamie was then transferred to a prison in Maryborough.

My mood began to lift, and I knew that, whatever happened, I had a relief from the stress for a short time. Sometimes, James being in prison was the only time I felt relieved from the constant worries, not because there was nothing to worry about, but that it wasn't all on my shoulders. I even began to reduce my anti-depressant to half a tablet.

Finally, on the 25th of November 2013, release day approached, and we were all excited. Jamie said he would be catching the bus on the highway near the prison, and would arrive in Caboolture sometime during the day. We agreed that he would drop into my work as soon as he arrived, which he did. I was so happy to see him, as always. He looked well and had his favourite tracksuit jacket on, brown with white stripes down the arms. I gave him a big hug and, as I had to get back to work, I said we would catch up when I finished work. I didn't see him for long Monday night, as he spent some time with his dad. I sent him a text asking if he was smoking pot downstairs. He came upstairs and let me know that he was just smoking rollies and that I must have forgotten the smell, and we had a laugh. He assured me he was not using anything.

Jamie was up early the next day, and said he had lots of things to do, like go to Centrelink. I dropped him off in Caboolture, and went to work. When I arrived home, he looked very glassy-eyed, but he assured me that he wasn't using only he felt tired, as he seemed to have become confused about the shortcuts he used to get around. He gave me his rent money (always the first thing he paid), and I left to go shopping. I did most of my shopping at Burpengary Plaza but, with $60 left over, I decided to drop in to Aldi. I stopped to look at some beach towels and placed my purse in the seat of the trolley while I checked out the towels. I headed off to the checkout and realised my purse was stolen. Staff were amazing and immediately checked

CCTV and checked the back of the store in case they had dropped the purse, but it couldn't be located. We searched all the bins, and I rang Jamie to let him know that I would be a while, as I had to report it to the police before I came home. I knew Grace had been asleep for hours, after all of the excitement of her end-of-year activities, and she was still asleep.

I arrived home and, luckily, most of the groceries had been purchased before the purse was stolen, so Jamie and I packed them away, chatting comfortably. We finally sat down in the lounge room, about 7pm, just on dark, and talked. Jamie says he is doing well, he's just very tired. He sounds upbeat and positive, and says he has an appointment with the Melaleuca Clinic the next morning, and how the staff are excited to see him. Melaleuca was the one service Jamie felt really understood him. They had been beside him on his journey over the past few years. Staff had also become supportive of me and the family, after initially struggling over confidentiality.

Jamie talked about feeling at peace, as if he had let all the trauma from the past go. We laughed over how the predictions over him dying in his teenage years had been off the mark and how "we showed them". We talked about his favourite artist, Eminem, and I played the new release *Monster*, a duet with Rhianna. He listened intently and said, "He has still got it," and we laughed.

Jamie said he was tired and wanted to be up for the appointment with Melaleuca. He asked if I could take him to train station in the morning, and I agree. He grabs some videos and says he will watch them before sleeping. I get up to hug him before he goes downstairs. As I release him, he looks at me, and I see a twinge of pain in his eyes as he says, "Lacey always blamed me for John's death." I reply, knowing that this is the truth. "It is hard when you lose someone you love not to look for someone to blame, but it wasn't your fault. You were just a boy, honey. You are not to blame." He nodded his head and walked downstairs. I feel so sad that this plays on his mind, so many years later.

I listen to music for a while before going to bed myself, and wake up at my usual time to get ready for work. Grace is still sleeping, so I leave her alone. I text Jamie to get up if he wants a lift, just as I have done many time times before. It's unusual, but he doesn't respond or hear me, like he usually does, and he doesn't get up to say hello. I am slightly concerned, but think about him looking so tired last night, so I prepare and go to work after sending another text that he doesn't respond to. I am not worried, as I had been in the past, when I knew he was using heavily, and I would go down to find him semi-conscious on the lounge and had to wake him to get him moving. No, none of that today. I am relaxed and not overly concerned. I sometimes wonder if that was my own protective instincts kicking in.

I go to work and send a text to his friend, Brett, asking him to check in on him, and give him a lift to the station if he could. Brett agrees. He texts back a short time later saying that the door was not open, and Jamie didn't answer, so we assume that he has gone to the 10am appointment already.

Around midday Grace rings me, as she had finally woken up. She had planned to go to her friend's place today for a sleepover, and is almost ready. I casually ask if she has seen Jamie. She says no, but she wanted to borrow his earphones, so was going to ask him. I hesitate, suddenly scared, but only momentarily, and say, "Okay." I stay on the phone while she goes downstairs. She comes back and says, "He is still asleep." I am relieved. Then she adds, "He is in a funny position." I freeze and know I need to get her out of there. It was like a veil had lifted and suddenly I knew he was gone. I distract her by saying, "Go upstairs and see if you can find my earphones. But, anyway, I will buy you some, just get going to the train station now."

I got off the phone and turned to my co-workers. "Jamie has collapsed. I need to go now."

I didn't wait for anyone's reaction. I grabbed my bag and rang his friend, Brett, telling him to go immediately to Jamie, as I thought he had collapsed. I made it across the road and was walking quickly down the ramp to the carpark when Brett called back.

"He's gone, Amanda. What do I do now?"

My mind wants to work. All I can do is say, "Call an ambulance, and get Grace out of there. Tell her to go to her friend's."

I am bent over with overwhelming pain, tears flowing. I turn back towards my office and, through blinding tears, call the office, telling the admin that I am across the road and Jamie is dead. She instructs me gently to make my way back to the office and someone will meet me downstairs.

Lacey works in the same office, and she guides me and helps me get to the car, driving me home, with the instruction that I have to let his dad know. I make the call, through my tears, and tell his disbelieving Dad who agrees to come to my home as soon as he can.

I arrived home, the ambulance in the driveway, and the beautiful ambulance officer offering her condolences. I couldn't acknowledge her or let her know I understood he was dead. as that would make it too real. Lacey went to the train station to get Grace where she was waiting, looking confused. She walks in the door and I grab her and tell her that Jamie is dead. She collapses to the floor wailing, "It can't be true! It can't be true!" She had heard the ambulances and knew something was wrong, but, like all of us, her mind fought against what was real.

The school was contacted for pastoral care for Grace, and they were an amazing support to all of the family. Police arrived to conduct the investigation, and Charlie identified Jamie's body, as I couldn't do it. One of the most horrific things that happened that day, and one that I will never ever forget, is a phone call I received from Probation and Parole. I was pacing, trying to calm myself, when the phone rang. A female asked, "Is Daniel there?" Thinking it was a mistake, I replied, "There is no Daniel here."

She countered with "Daniel. Your son, Daniel."

My anger rose. "My son's name is James."

"Oh, that's it, James. He hasn't attended to his reporting."

I try to remain calm and tell her that "he has died."

Obviously shocked, she apologises and hangs up.

A few minutes later, I get another call from her. "We have no record of him passing away. When did this happen?"

This time, I am less that polite. "That might be as the police are here still investigating. It might take some time till a record is made."

Shockingly, she accuses, "Are you sure?"

I scream, "What you think? I am making this is up? What you think? He is going to skip parole? Leave the state?... He is dead!" And hung up.

I don't remember the order, but the priest comes to bless Jamie. I tell his Dad to pull a bit of his hair from the top of his head, as the Buddhists believe this releases the spirit after death.

Police talk about ruling it suicide, and I say I don't think that this was the case, but am unsure. They tell me there is a suicide note, but refuse to allow me to see it. Grace's Deputy Principal, an amazing lady, challenges his authority to keep Jamie's personal items from me. He relents and lets Lacey read it, but not me. It is part of the evidence, so is removed from the home.

Jamie leaves his forever home for the last time, and part of me hopes that he is at peace now, as I know that his pain has stopped. I was given a Buddhist book about life, living and death. In it, I read that, if you mediate every night for the first 47 days after someone's death, you can help them in their spiritual journey, and keep them protected. In those early days, it gave me comfort that I was still able to provide him love and care, and help him.

Epilogue

Sharing My Lessons

These days, I have a clear image of who I am, but that has not come easily. As I enter my fifties, I have accepted myself as I am, for all my faults, for all the traits of Borderline Personality Disorder that I carry, and for the damage I unknowingly have inflicted on others, especially my children. Throughout my life I have tried to make up for this in my actions towards others. I have tried to be compassionate and empathetic, and I have strived to at least make some small changes, as a positive legacy to my family and future generations.

I am married to a beautiful Indonesian man who stands beside me now as I continue to provide a place of safety for my children, grandchildren and other family. He is a man who is very religious and has a strong sense of who he is. He brings a lot of joy back to my life with his humour, stability and sense of fun. I look forward to many more years, perhaps some where we will have more time for ourselves.

After Jamie died, I didn't want to be in Australia on the anniversaries of his death or on his birthday. I went to Bali and met my now-husband there, and he talked and joked with me each day. He asked to meet my dad, and asked my father's permission to date me. I converted to Islam and we went to Java and had a religious ceremony. In July 2017 he came to Australia on a partner visa, and we got legally married. He is on a bridging visa now, and we have applied for permanent residency status. Still, nothing I plan ever happens; I thought I'd be on my own for the rest of my life. He brings me lots of joy and makes me very happy. He really misses his family and travels back to java when he can.

It is often said that I have an extraordinary understanding of mental illness. It is instinctively that I know what is required to support people, even if they are resistant or opposed, and I have found that most people respond to my heartfelt attempts to improve their lives or that of their children.

As for my own children, Chantel still lives in Bunbury in Western Australia, and despite her children having grown up in out-of-home care, she also has done her best to maintain a connection to them. Her mental health is somewhat more settled these days, but she is still at a stage where just surviving is the main focus. She has endured immeasurable trauma, including extreme domestic violence, the loss of her children, and grief for her child, her brother, a beautiful Indigenous mentor, and, more recently, her father. During my last call with her she was clear, yet lost, but still not wanting to come home. Not since early adolescence has there been conflict between us. I survived the fears that she would be murdered by her partner, or that her lifestyle would end in her death. She has shared the many attempts at suicide that she has made that were unsuccessful. Years ago, we made peace with her thoughts that I, as a mother, had tried hard, but just didn't know how to help her.

Chantel's six children all keep in contact with me occasionally via Facebook, and her oldest daughter has visited us and stayed at times when she has been unwell, homeless, and a victim of domestic violence. She has been diagnosed with Schizoid Affective Disorder, and she comes to us and stays until she is stronger, before returning to Western Australia. On two occasions, hospitals have talked to me about how she is not unwell enough to stay in hospital, but that releasing her to a dysfunctional community has a negative effect on her – and we love having her with us. All the grandchildren suffer from some form of mental illness, and all struggle with suicidal thoughts or self-harm.

Jade struggled for many years and found solace in alcohol and substance abuse from trauma including a traumatic sexual assault, bankruptcy due to her gambling addiction, loss of custody of her children, and the loss of her brother. At that stage, I watched as she declined even further into alcoholism, and I feared for her life. She made it through, she found faith, attended rehab, and is now set in the Salvation Army, looking forward to becoming an officer. Her faith has provided her the opportunity to assist those struggling with mental illness or addictions, and she has an astonishing gift to heal.

James died of what was determined in the coroner's report, six months later, as hypertrophic cardiomyopathy, possibly heredity in nature, but certainly impacted by his lifestyle choices. He left a huge hole in my life, and, as is often noted, the death of a child changes one forever – you can never go back to being the same person again. I went through all the usual grief emotions and attempted to focus on finding a way to make what happened have some positive meaning. I struggled with the systems, such as health, education and legal institutions, who made our journey much tougher than it needed to be at times.

I harboured anger towards the police that had so brutally beaten my son and acted to cover their actions. I overcame this by reminding myself of their humanity and, on what would have been Jamie's 30th birthday, I presented the local police station with a birthday cake and a thank you card for those who had assisted me when I was unsafe.

Grace, my beautiful gift, despite her diagnosis, is functioning well, for the most part. She works really hard as a dental assistant, and has found herself a beautiful partner who understands her struggles and treats her with compassion, love and tenderness. Her fears of abandonment still impact her, and she works on this when she can.

My mum is settled back in an aged care home in Western Australia, after a decision was made collaboratively between the Public Guardian and family to move her back to her community in Western Australia.

On the weekend recently, my daughter was talking to mum on the phone. Jade and her daughter began singing "Amazing Grace" to Mum, and Mum began to scream. *Did she like it?* They wondered.

"I loved it!" She said, clear as day.

The screaming was her inability to manage her emotions. She couldn't manage her intense feelings; she could only scream. It's hard to live with mental illness when your connection to the person is so great. There are many incidents like that.

I think that another of my strengths was that I had strong, long-lasting relationships that sustained me through tough times. My friendships assisted me to cope, and I learned other ways of being a parent. I often reflect how BPD affects the ability to maintain relationships, and that it's probably the most painful trait, as sufferers need so much support, but can get caught in sabotaging relationships without intending to, further isolating themselves. Usually, they are great people who attract friends easily, but are unsure or unable to maintain lasting, quality relationships. This is the cruel irony of Borderline Personality Disorder.

My experience was unusual during the time when I was parenting, but I see a huge increase in vulnerable families, as the rates of mental illness and suicide among young people rise at tremendous rates. Combine this with the high rate of addiction impacting consecutive generations, and we have a compounding of complex issues impacting society.

I believe that we've created this society where both parents need to work, without the supports needed, and there lies some of the problems. Parents are so worn-out that they are losing their ability to create true attachments with their children. We can identify these families easily. Every mother who is in mental health care should be supported automatically. Every child in that family will absolutely be impacted.

Our systems are struggling to respond to the need, and there is not a willingness to change. Our prisons are full of people suffering disability or mental illness — many whose incarceration can be related to substance abuse.

I became a consumer representative around mental health and addiction issues, and I look forward to a time that I don't have to work full-time so that I can give more time to this work. I continue to work with families. I have a great deal of experience in child protection, youth justice, and youth crime prevention, supporting families before they hit crisis point. It's very intensive work, taking them to parks and teaching them how to enjoy having fun together as a family.

I reflect on how people with a history of trauma enter professions with the aim of helping others. People damaged by trauma enter the care professions because they can best connect with other traumatised people, and this is as it should be. But they themselves need support to be able to continue to do such important work.